Cambridge Elements

Elements in the Philosophy of Mathematics
edited by
Penelope Rush
University of Tasmania
Stewart Shapiro
The Ohio State University

PHILOSOPHICAL USES OF CATEGORICITY ARGUMENTS

Penelope Maddy
University of California

Jouko Väänänen
University of Helsinki

CAMBRIDGE
UNIVERSITY PRESS

Shaftesbury Road, Cambridge CB2 8EA, United Kingdom

One Liberty Plaza, 20th Floor, New York, NY 10006, USA

477 Williamstown Road, Port Melbourne, VIC 3207, Australia

314–321, 3rd Floor, Plot 3, Splendor Forum, Jasola District Centre,
New Delhi – 110025, India

103 Penang Road, #05–06/07, Visioncrest Commercial, Singapore 238467

Cambridge University Press is part of Cambridge University Press & Assessment,
a department of the University of Cambridge.

We share the University's mission to contribute to society through the pursuit of
education, learning and research at the highest international levels of excellence.

www.cambridge.org
Information on this title: www.cambridge.org/9781009467964

DOI: 10.1017/9781009432894

First published 2023

A catalogue record for this publication is available from the British Library

ISBN 978-1-009-46796-4 Hardback
ISBN 978-1-009-43292-4 Paperback
ISSN 2514-2883 (online)
ISSN 2514-3808 (print)

Philosophical Uses of Categoricity Arguments

Elements in the Philosophy of Mathematics

DOI: 10.1017/9781009432894
First published online: December 2023

Penelope Maddy
University of California

Jouko Väänänen
University of Helsinki

Author for correspondence: Penelope Maddy, pjmaddy@uci.edu

Abstract: This Element addresses the viability of categoricity arguments in philosophy by focusing with some care on the specific conclusions that a sampling of prominent figures have attempted to draw – the same theorem might successfully support one such conclusion while failing to support another. It begins historically, with Dedekind, Zermelo, and Kreisel, casting doubt on received readings of the latter two and highlighting the success of all three in achieving what are argued to be their actual goals. These earlier uses of categoricity arguments are then compared and contrasted with the more recent work of Parsons and the coauthors Button and Walsh. Highlighting the roles of first- and second-order theorems, of external and (two varieties of) internal theorems, the Element eventually concludes that categoricity arguments have been more effective in historical cases that reflect philosophically on internal mathematical matters than in more recent uses for questions of pre-theoretic metaphysics.

Keywords: categoricity, second-order logic, philosophy of mathematics, set theory, history of logic

JEL classifications: A12, B34, C56, D78, E90

ISBNs: 9781009467964 (HB), 9781009432924 (PB), 9781009432894 (OC)
ISSNs: 2514-2883 (online), 2514-3808 (print)

Contents

1 Introduction

Mathematicians and philosophers have appealed to categoricity arguments in a surprisingly varied range of contexts. One familiar example calls on second-order categoricity in an attempt to show that the Continuum Hypothesis, despite its formal independence, has a determinate truth value, but this doesn't exhaust the uses of categoricity even in set theory, not to mention its appearance in various roles in discussions of arithmetic. Here, we compare and contrast a sampling of these deployments to get a sense of when these arguments tend to succeed and when they tend to fail. Our story begins with two historical landmarks, Dedekind and Zermelo, on arithmetic and set theory, respectively, and ends with leading contemporary writers, Charles Parsons and the coauthors Tim Button and Sean Walsh, again on arithmetic and set theory, respectively. In between, we pause over the well-known contribution of Georg Kreisel. In each case,[1] we ask: What does the author set out to accomplish, philosophically? What do they actually do (or what can be done), mathematically? And does what's done (or can be done) accomplish what they set out to do? We find this focus on context illuminating: these authors have qualitatively different philosophical goals, and what works for one might not work for another.

2 Dedekind in "Was sind und was sollen die Zahlen?" (1888)

2.1 What Does He Set Out to Accomplish?

Dedekind's motivation for his treatment of natural numbers in "Was sind und was sollen die Zahlen" (Dedekind, 1888) is explicit: "in science nothing capable of proof ought to be believed without proof" (p. 790).[2] Ideally, such a proof should not depend on the vagaries of geometric intuition or temporal intuition or anything of that sort; rather, the "number-concept" and the resulting proofs should emerge as "an immediate product of the pure laws of thought" (pp. 790–791). This is what Dedekind means when he says that "arithmetic [is] merely a part of logic" (p. 790), so it's important to note that these "pure laws of thought" include what we would regard as set formation: "It very frequently happens that different things, a, b, c, . . . for some reason can be considered from a common point of view, can be associated in the mind, and we say that they form a *system*." (section 2, p. 797).

---

[1] With the exception of Section 4, where no new mathematics is involved.

[2] Unless otherwise indicated, all references in this section are to the English translation of Dedekind (1888) in Ewald (2005, pp. 796–833).

(Of course, a "system" here is what we'd call a "set.") In sum, then, Dedekind is out to show that the concept of number can be characterized and the theorems of arithmetic proved using only logical notions, in his generous sense of "logical." This would complete the project, initiated in Dedekind (1872), of founding the calculus and higher analysis without appeal to geometric or temporal intuition.[3]

2.2 What Does He Actually Do?

Dedekind begins by articulating some of his logical laws of thought, in particular, some pre-theoretic metaphysical truths about sets.[4] The most important of these, obviously, is the above-noted assumption that "very frequently" some things "can be considered from a common point of view" and thus collected into a set. (If this isn't Unlimited Comprehension, Dedekind tells us nothing about how it differs; only later does he recognize the danger [see Section 2.3].) From there, he develops an early theory of sets: extensionality and the existence of singletons (section 2), unions (section 8), and intersections of families (§17). He introduces functions ("mappings", section 21) as entities distinct from sets, assumes that identity functions exist, that the restriction of a function to a subset is still a function, and that functions can be composed (implicitly).

He then introduces the key idea of a "ϕ-chain" (section 37)[5]:

Definition 1   *If ϕ is a function from S to S, and $K \subseteq S$, then K is a ϕ-chain iff $\forall x \in K(\phi(x) \in K)$.*

This notion in hand, Dedekind defines

---

[3] The weak set theory of Dedekind (1888) is enough for the construction of reals via Dedekind cuts in Dedekind (1872).

[4] Fortunately, difficult questions about the status of these sets – for example, are they understood realistically or idealistically? – can be set aside for present purposes.

[5] Dedekind (n.d., pp. 100–101) explains the importance of this notion to his critic, Keferstein, who thought it could be eliminated. Dedekind points out that a simply infinite system, (N, a, ϕ), could be contained in a larger system, S, with some "arbitrary additional elements t, to which the mapping ϕ" could be applied and a subset, T, containing t and closed under ϕ. The question is how "to cleanse our system S . . . of such alien intruders t as disturb every vestige of order and to restrict it to N?" We might try saying "an element n belongs to the sequence N if and only if, starting with the element [a] and counting on and on steadfastly . . . through a finite number of iterations of the mapping ϕ . . . I actually reach the element n . . . But this . . . would . . . contain the most pernicious and obvious kind of vicious circle. . . Thus, how can I, without presupposing any arithmetic knowledge, give an unambiguous conceptual foundation to the distinction between the elements n and the elements t? Merely through consideration of *chains* . . . and . . . by means of these, completely!" He notes that Frege's ancestral "agrees in *essence* with my notion of chain . . . only, one must not be put off by his somewhat inconvenient terminology."

Definition 2 *S is* simply infinite *iff there is a one-to-one ϕ from S to S and an s ∈ S such that*

1. *there is no x ∈ S with ϕ(x) = s,*
2. *S = ⋂{X | s ∈ X and X is a ϕ-chain}.*

By this point, he's defined Dedekind-infinite and proved that there's an infinite set in the notorious section 66: the collection of "all things which can be objects of my thought" is infinite because a function that sends each element therein to the thought of that element in fact maps the set to a proper subset of itself (at least one element is not a thought, "e.g., my own ego")! He then shows that every infinite set contains a simply infinite set.

So, finally, where are the numbers? Here Dedekind abstracts:

> If in the consideration of a simply infinite system *N* ordered by a mapping *ϕ* we entirely neglect the special character of the elements, simply retaining their distinguishability and taking into account only the relations to one another in which they are placed by the ordering mapping *ϕ*, then these elements are called *natural numbers*. (section 73, p. 809)

The precise ontological status of these numbers won't concern us here, but for the record they are "a free creation of the human mind" (section 73, p. 809).[6]

The so-called Peano Axioms, more properly the Dedekind–Peano Axioms, are implicit in the definition of simply infinite: if *S* is simply infinite, with *ϕ* from *S* to *S* and *s* ∈ *S* satisfying the above conditions, then *A* ⊆ *S*, *s* ∈ *A*, and *A* closed under *ϕ* implies *A* = *S*. With the axioms in place, the usual theorems of arithmetic follow and "are always the same in all ordered simply infinite systems, whatever names may happen to be given to the individual elements" (section 73, p. 809).

This is certainly true – the consequences of PA hold in all relevant systems – but it isn't enough to guarantee that performing the process of abstraction described in the previous paragraph on different simply infinite systems won't generate different natural numbers. Apparently sensitive to this loose end, Dedekind refers us forward to his proofs that any simply infinite set is isomorphic to the numbers (section 132) and that any set isomorphic to the numbers is simply infinite (section 133). Thus, the simply infinite systems form an isomorphism class (section 34), so it doesn't matter which one he happens to abstract from in section 73. Only then, in section 134, does he conclude that "the definition of the notion of numbers given in section 73 is fully justified" (section 134,

---

[6] Exactly what Dedekind intends by "free creation" is beside the point for our purposes, but it is a fascinating question. See Reck (2003) and Sieg and Morris (2018) for quite different readings.

p. 823). This is the role of his famous categoricity result in the overall project of showing that the natural numbers can be characterized without appeal to intuition, in purely logical terms.

So, how does the proof go? Averting our gaze from "free creations," we sketch a direct Dedekind-style proof that any two simply infinite sets are isomorphic:

Theorem 1 *Suppose N and N' are simply infinite, that is, that there are $a \in N$ and $a' \in N'$ and one-one functions $\phi: N \rightarrow N$, and $\phi': N' \rightarrow N'$ such that there is no $x \in N$ nor $x' \in N'$ with $\phi(x) = a$ or $\phi(x') = a'$, and*

$$N = \bigcap \{X: a \in X \text{ and } X \text{ is a } \phi\text{-chain}\}, \tag{2.1}$$

and

$$N' = \bigcap \{X: a' \in X \text{ and } X \text{ is a } \phi'\text{-chain}\}, \tag{2.2}$$

then $N \cong N'$.

Proof:

Suppose N and N' are as above. To construct an isomorphism between (N, ϕ, a) and (N', ϕ', a'), proceed by induction in N: for $b \in N$, define ψ_b, an isomorphism from b and its predecessors into N' such that $\psi_b(a) = a'$ and $\psi_b(\phi(x)) = \phi'(\psi_b(x))$ (section 125). Then let $\psi(b) = \psi_b(b)$ (section 126), and show, by induction on N', that ψ is onto N'. The required isomorphism is ψ (section 132). □

2.3 Does What He Did Accomplish What He Set Out to Do?

It seems fair to say that Dedekind has achieved his goal of characterizing the natural numbers without appeal to geometric or temporal intuition, but from our contemporary perspective, it's impossible to ignore the freedom with which he allows "different things" to be "considered from a common point of view [and] associated in the mind" so as to form a set (section 2, p. 797). Dedekind reports that the dangers of this free use of comprehension came clear to him in 1903 and troubled him so much that he was at first reluctant to allow a third edition of his little book:

> When I was asked . . . to replace the second edition of this work (which was already out of print) by a third, I had misgivings about doing so, because in the meantime doubts had arisen about the reliability of important foundations of my conception. Even today I do not underestimate the importance, and to some extent the correctness, of these doubts. (Dedekind, 1888, p. 796)

Still, though he was "prevented by other tasks from completing such an investigation," Dedekind remains confident:

> My trust in the inner harmony of our logic is not ... shattered; I believe that a rigorous investigation of the power of the mind to create from determinate elements a new determinate, their system, that is necessarily different from each of these elements, will certainly lead to an unobjectionable formulation of the foundations of my work. (p. 796)

As we know, he turned out to be right about this.

Of course, any way of regularizing Dedekind's reasoning to contemporary standards will inevitably distort it in some way. Two methods appear in the literature – one set-theoretic, one second-order – with the latter perhaps more common. To assess the moral of Dedekind's work for ourselves today, we look at each of these in turn.

The first is fairly direct. Dedekind's presentation is already formulated in an early set-theoretic context; the only problem is his assumption of what looks perilously close to Unlimited Comprehension. In his categoricity theorem, this comes into play when he forms the family of all ϕ-chains containing a (N is its intersection). In fact, though, this isn't problematic, because all those ϕ-chains are subsets of N, so the relevant family can be generated by Separation from $\mathcal{P}(N)$. On closer inspection, the relevant intersection can be formulated as ...

$$\{x \in N: \forall y((\forall z \in y(z \in N) \land a \in y \land \forall z \in y(s(z) \in y)) \to x \in y)\}.$$

... so only Π_1^1-Separation is needed. Beyond that, we know today that much weaker principles suffice: Simpson and Yokoyama (2013) show that WKL_0 (Weak König's Lemma[7]) suffices over RCA_0 (Recursive Comprehension Axiom). This is interesting because WKL_0 is weaker than Peano arithmetic itself (i.e., ACA_0).

In the second, more common reading, Dedekind's reasoning is cast, not set-theoretically, but as proving the categoricity of second-order Peano Arithmetic.[8] The conditions on simply infinite sets are then replaced by the second-order Peano Axioms, and Theorem 1 becomes:

Theorem 2 *Suppose $(N, S, 0) \models PA^2$ and $(N', S', 0') \models PA^2$, where N and N' are full models.[9] Then there is a bijection $f: N \to N'$ such that*

---

[7] Every infinite binary subtree of $2^{<\omega}$ has an infinite branch.

[8] See, for example Shapiro (1991, pp. 82–83) and Button and Walsh (2018, p. 155).

[9] A second-order model is *full* if it interprets the second-order variables as ranging over the full power set of the domain – as opposed to a *Henkin model*, which only needs enough subsets to satisfy the axioms of second-order logic (comprehension and choice).

$$f(0_N) = 0_{N'},$$
$$f(S_N(x)) = S_{N'}(f(x)),$$

that is, $f: N \cong N'$.

Dedekind's proof easily translates to treat models of PA^2 instead of simply infinite sets, but it still takes place within his set-theoretic background theory.

Though the two readings don't differ in their underlying mathematical content, the contrast between them is worth noting. In Theorem 1, the conditions on a "simply infinite" set are stated directly: for example, there is no $x \in N$ such that $S(x) = 0$. In Theorem 2, those same conditions appear indirectly: in the same example, N satisfies the axiom "there is no x such that $S(x) = 0$." The latter involves semantic notions, while the former does not; as a philosopher might put it, the former uses the set-theoretic conditions, while the latter only mentions them.[10] As we'll use the terms, Theorem 1 is a *weakly internal* categoricity argument and Theorem 2 is *external*.[11] Despite the apparent preference in the literature for the external reading, the weakly internal reading strikes us as considerably closer to Dedekind's own thought, but either way, the main moral we wish to draw remains: Dedekind has successfully achieved his goal; he's shown that the natural numbers can be described without appeal to geometric or temporal intuition.

3 Zermelo in "On Boundary Numbers and Domains Of Sets" (1930c)

3.1 What Does He Set Out to Accomplish?

Perhaps the first thing to note about the aims of this well-known paper (Zermelo, 1930c) is that Zermelo isn't out to do what many recent observers have imagined; he isn't out to introduce the iterative hierarchy, to argue that the axioms are true therein, and to use this purported fact to motivate or defend the truth of ZFC. In fact, the paper moves in the opposite direction, beginning with a list of the axioms and arguing that any model thereof – any "normal domain" – can be stratified into well-ordered ranks, into V_α's. In a subsequent report back to his funding agency on what he's done so far, Zermelo catalogs the benefits of this analysis and proposes, as a distinct continuation, the project of constructing "a set-theoretic model" (Zermelo, 1930a, p. 441). A subsequent sketch (Zermelo, 1930b) indicates what he has in mind – laying out a

---

[10] For those unfamiliar with this terminology, the word "cat" is *used* in the sentence: the cat is on the mat. It's *mentioned* in the sentence: the word "cat" has three letters.

[11] *Strongly internal* or just *internal* will be introduced and eventually formalized in Section 5.2.

pre-theoretic iterative picture and arguing that the axioms are true there – but his stated goal even then is to establish the consistency of the axioms, not their truth. So we need to look a bit more closely at his intentions in "On boundary numbers" (Zermelo, 1930c).

The only aim mentioned in the opening paragraph of the paper is the resolution of the paradoxes:

> it is this sharp distinction between the different models of the . . . axiom system that allows us to resolve the 'ultrafinite antinomies' (Zermelo, 1930c, p. 29[401])[12]

This was also an explicit aim of his original axiomatization in Zermelo (1908b)[13]:

> In solving the problem [of axiomatization] we must, on the one hand, restrict these principles sufficiently to exclude all contradictions and, on the other, take them sufficiently wide to retain all that is valuable in this theory. (Zermelo, 1908b, p. 191[200])[14]

But he was clearly dissatisfied with the resolution given there:

> I have not yet been able to prove rigorously that my axioms are 'consistent', though this is certainly very essential; instead I have had to confine myself to pointing out now and then that the 'antinomies' discovered so far vanish one and all if the principles here proposed are adopted as a basis. (Zermelo, 1908b, p. 191[200–201])

So at least one goal of Zermelo (1930c) is to provide a broader and more explanatory treatment of the paradoxes.

It's also worth noting the second clause in the first quotation above from Zermelo (1908b): "sufficiently wide to retain all that is valuable in this theory." Zermelo's eye is always on the mathematical powers of his assumptions; in his Zermelo (1908a), for example – the "new proof" of well-ordering, companion

---

[12] The first page reference is to the original publication in *Fundamenta Mathematica*, the second to the English translation in Zermelo (2010).

[13] Moore (1982, pp.159–160) points out that Zermelo intended his early axiomatization to bolster his proof of the well-ordering theorem by clearly isolating the assumptions required. Ebbinghaus (2007, pp. 76–79) acknowledges this goal, but places Zermelo's early efforts squarely in the larger context of Hilbert's foundational project, where axiomatization and consistency proofs were central – obviously a reaction to the paradoxes. In fact, Zermelo was inclined to withhold publication of his Zermelo (1908b) until he had the desired consistency proof, but Hilbert, out of concern for his young colleague's immediate career prospects, advised him not to wait. As noted above, Zermelo continued to pursue a consistency proof in the 1930s.

[14] Page references in Zermelo (1908a) and (1908b) are to the reprinting in Zermelo (2010), followed by the reprinting in van Heijenoort (1967).

to Zermelo (1908b) – he defends the axiom of choice on the basis of its theoretical benefits:

> Principles must be judged from the point of view of science [i.e., mathematics], and not science from the point of view of principles fixed once and for all. (Zermelo, 1908a, p. 135[189])

Zermelo takes it as obvious that there is much of mathematical value in infinitary set theory and that axioms can be properly assessed in terms of the mathematical achievements they enable. (These are so-called extrinsic justifications, which Zermelo pioneered.[15]) So we should also expect some discussion of the mathematical consequences of the axioms he considers.

3.2 What Does He Actually Do?

Like Dedekind, Zermelo works in a pre-theoretic background theory of sets,[16] but unlike Dedekind, he doesn't make this explicit. (The content of that background theory is inferred from his argumentation in what follows.) He begins, instead, by listing the axioms of the theory he'll be studying. Extensionality, Separation, Pairing, Power Set, and Union carry over from Zermelo (1908b). Infinity is omitted "because it does not belong to 'general' set theory" (Zermelo, 1930c, p. 30[403]), an omission whose rationale emerges only later in the paper.[17] Choice is now regarded, not as a set-theoretic axiom, but as "a general logical principle upon which our entire investigation is based" (Zermelo, 1930c, p. 31[405]), giving us our first glimpse of what's true in Zermelo's implicit background theory. Finally, the explicit list is supplemented by Replacement,[18] attributed to Fraenkel, and Foundation. Of course, the property in Separation and the function in Replacement are to be understood as "unrestricted" or "arbitrary," what we now think of as second-order, and Kanamori points out that Foundation, too, must be second-order in the absence of Infinity.[19] This system Zermelo calls ZF'.

Little is said in defense of this selection of axioms. This is understandable for the carry-over axioms, as they were treated in Zermelo (1908a) and Zermelo (1908b), and perhaps it was fair to assume that the case for Replacement has already been aired in the literature, for example, by Fraenkel and von

---

[15] For the record, extrinsic considerations weigh the mathematical benefits of a claim, as opposed to its intrinsic obviousness or connection to the concept of set. See, for example, Maddy (2011).
[16] Once again (cf. footnote 4), we set aside questions about the metaphysical nature of these sets.
[17] See footnote 32.
[18] Zermelo notes the redundancy this introduces.
[19] See Kanamori (2010b, pp. 393–394).

Neumann.[20] The one comment Zermelo does make concerns the new axiom of Foundation:

> This last axiom, which excludes all 'circular' sets, all 'self-membered' sets in particular, and all 'rootless' sets in general, has always been satisfied in all practical applications of set theory, and, hence, does not result in an essential restriction of the theory for the time being.[21] (Zermelo, 1930c, p. 31[403])

So Foundation is benign, at least as far as currently understood, and perhaps there is some intuitive appeal to ruling out "pathological" sets, but the full case in its defense only comes later (see Section 3.3).

Zermelo then introduces the central object of his study:

> We call '*normal domain*' a domain of 'sets' and 'urelements' that satisfies our 'ZF'-system' with regard to the 'basic relation' $a \in b$. (Zermelo, 1930c, p. 31[405])

To the contemporary ear, this sounds like a model satisfying the theory, but Zermelo isn't working with a syntax/semantics distinction.[22] To begin with, "$\in$" isn't to be reinterpreted: the $\in$ of the normal domain is the $\in$ of the background theory.[23] The same is true for the second-order quantifiers: $N \models$ Separation^2 (where Separation^2 is second-order Separation) allows for sparse Henkin-style interpretations of the second-order quantifier; Zermelo claims, instead, that for every property P and every set $x \in N$, there is a set $y \in N$ containing just the members of x with P, where the relevant properties include all subsets of N as understood in the background theory. Or, to take another example, for N to satisfy Power Set in Zermelo's sense is for N to include $\mathcal{P}(a)$ for every

---

[20] Though see footnote 36.

[21] It's not clear to us what work Zermelo's many quotation marks are intended to do here and elsewhere, so we pass them by without further comment.

[22] Cf. Ebbinghaus (2007, pp. 182–183), describing Zermelo's discussion of "definite properties" in 1929:

> there is no sharp distinction between language and meaning. In fact, Zermelo will never be clear on this point. His negligence will have a major impact in later discussions with Gödel. The separation of syntax and semantics or – more adequately – its methodological control became the watershed that separated the area of the "classic" researchers such as Zermelo and Fraenkel from the domain of the "new" foundations as developed by younger researchers, among them Gödel, Skolem, and von Neumann.

[23] From a modern point of view, we can see that if $(M, R) \models$ ZF', which includes second-order Foundation, then it's isomorphic to the $\in$-model generated by a Mostowski collapse. So the fact that Zermelo doesn't entertain such reinterpretation is ultimately less significant than it might seem.

$a \in N$, where that's the real $\mathcal{P}(a)$, as judged from the perspective of the background theory. Zermelo's normal domains are what we'd call *full* models of the second-order axioms.[24]

With the axioms and the notion of normal domain in place, Zermelo begins his study by introducing the von Neumann ordinals, starting not from the empty set but from an arbitrary urelement: $u, \{u\}, \{u, \{u\}\}, \ldots$. Working in the background theory here, he's implicitly relying on Pairing. Moments later, Union is applied to define the successor of the αth u-based ordinal, g_α, as $g_\alpha \cup \{g_\alpha\}$, but more importantly, this happens in the course of a definition by recursion – revealing that versions of all the ZF' axioms, including Replacement, are present in the background theory (with the possible exception of Foundation, see Section 3.3). The collection of all ordinals in a given normal domain, N, is itself an ordinal, though not an ordinal in N. This ordinal is called the "characteristic" or "boundary number" of N, and Zermelo proves that it must be a (strongly) inaccessible cardinal.

From here, the path to the theorem of interest is direct. It takes one lemma:

Lemma 1   *If N is a normal domain, $N' \subseteq N$ with the same urelements, and*

1. *N' is transitive, and*
2. *$A \subseteq N'$ and $A \in N \rightarrow A \in N'$,*

then $N' = N$.

This is where Foundation (in N) makes its essential appearance (in a proof by contradiction from the assumption that $N - N'$ is nonempty).[25]

Now suppose N is a normal domain with boundary number κ. Then let

$$N_0 = \text{the urelements of } N,$$
$$N_{\alpha+1} = N_\alpha \cup \mathcal{P}(N_\alpha),$$
$$N_\nu = \bigcup_{\beta < \nu} N_\beta, \text{ for limit } \nu < \kappa.$$

Given this familiar stratification on N into ranks, all that's left to show is that it exhausts N:

Theorem 3 $\bigcup_{\alpha < \kappa} N_\alpha = N.$

---

[24] Recall footnote 9.

[25] This is also where Kanamori (2010b, pp. 393–394) locates the second-order axiom. Recall footnote 19.

Now $\bigcup_{\alpha<\kappa} N_\alpha \subseteq N$, and $\bigcup_{\alpha<\kappa} N_\alpha$ and N have the same urelements by definition, so the lemma applies. The proof naturally uses the fact that κ is inaccessible.

This sets up the central theorem:

Theorem 4   *If N and N' are normal domains with the same boundary number and equinumerous urelements, then $N \cong N'$.*

The proof begins from a bijection of the urelements of N to the urelements of N' and builds an isomorphism from N to N' in stages for each rank N_α of N in a way that's now familiar to observers of set-theoretic categoricity arguments.

Several observations are in order about Zermelo's line of thought here. To begin with, though he himself uses the term, this isn't really a categoricity theorem in the sense in use today: "$\in$" isn't given different interpretations in N and N'. In fact, if the urelements are eliminated, the result reduces to the elementary fact, familiar from Set Theory 101, that any $\in$-model of ZF^2 is a V_κ, for some inaccessible κ. If you asked Zermelo, he'd no doubt insist that this is proved in (what we regard as) a second-order background theory, but all that actually matters is that N and N' satisfy the second-order ZF' – ordinary, first-order ZFC is enough in the background; in fact, ZFC restricted to Σ_2-separation and Σ_2-replacement will do (see Barwise, 1972).

So, ironically, what's made Zermelo's proof a touchstone in the contemporary literature on categoricity arguments is the presence of those urelements. Because those of N and N' are only equinumerous, not identical, the isomorphism isn't the identity – it has to be constructed rank by rank, from the initial bijection. Though Zermelo doesn't reinterpret "$\in$," he could have done so with essentially the same proof, which is why many commentators[26] take him to have proved the following theorem about second-order ZFC (ZFC^2):

Theorem 5   *If $N \models ZFC^2$ and $N' \models ZFC^2$, where N and N' are full models with the same height and equinumerous urelements, then $N \cong N'$.*

Actually, as with Dedekind, it's probably more faithful to see him as having proved Theorem 4 in his background theory of sets. In any case, from there he goes on to observe that if two normal domains have the same urelements, then one is isomorphic to an initial segment of the other, and that normal domains starting from the same single urelement (as $\emptyset$) stack neatly in the order of their boundary numbers.

---

[26] See, for example, Hellman (1989, pp. 66–67) and Button and Walsh (2018, pp. 178–179).

3.3 Does What He Did Accomplish What He Set Out to Do?

To answer this question, we need to follow Zermelo's line of thought a bit further. Working in his background theory,[27] he's shown that there's effectively one normal domain of each height, that each of these breaks down into ranks – essentially the theorem $V = \bigcup_{\alpha \in Ord} V_\alpha$,[28] – and that they form a hierarchy matching that of their boundary numbers. These mathematical facts suggest an image of the universe of sets as an endless series of neatly stratified domains. This image quickly grew into a compelling intuitive picture of emphatic richness,[29, 30] the Iterative Conception:

> We believe that the collection of all ordinals is very 'long' and that each
> power set (of an infinite set) is very 'thick'. (Wang, 1974, p. 553)

This picture suggests new methods like reflection and maximality arguments, new axioms like large cardinal and forcing axioms, along with all manner of elaborations and analyses.[31] Zermelo would insist on judging each resulting mathematical proposal by its extrinsic mathematical merits, and there's little doubt that he'd regard the Iterative Conception in this heuristic use as an impressive source of productive mathematical ideas.

All very good, one might say, but what if there are no boundary numbers? Zermelo addresses this question directly in the final section of the paper, beginning with the observation that the hereditarily finite sets form a normal domain that even the intuitionist would accept.[32] The trouble with stopping here, he goes on to note, is that it doesn't permit "Cantorian set theory," and thus would not, in words going back to 1908, "retain all that is valuable in this theory" (Zermelo, 1908b, p. 191[200]). This was Zermelo's extrinsic justification back then, and it remains so now: he includes the existence of ω, the boundary number of the normal domain of hereditarily finite sets, and the larger normal domain that contains it. Only a domain that satisfies ZF′+Infinity deserves to be called "Cantorian."

---

[27] Setting urelements aside.

[28] This notation just means: $\forall x \exists \alpha (x \in V_\alpha)$.

[29] This includes the combinatorial ideas of Bernays (1935).

[30] Boolos (1971) is an outlier. His austere version of the Iterative Conception doesn't include replacement – which many would regard as the first affirmation, after the axiom of infinity, that the sequence of ordinals is "very long" – or choice – which many would regard as an affirmation that the power set is "very thick" (see Bernays, 1935, p. 260).

[31] In a striking example, Bowler (2019, section 18.3) argues that the iterative picture "isn't just a nice extra feature that allows set theory lecturers to draw pretty pictures on the board," rather "it is vital" (p. 402): "Humans are adapted to build complex tools, which means building up objects from component parts, themselves built from yet simpler components" (p. 403).

[32] Now we see why Zermelo leaves Infinity off the list ZF′.

Notice that Zermelo isn't advocating that we add Infinity to ZF'; he's advocating that we add it to the background theory, to the theory that determines which normal domains there are and what they're like. In that background theory, he claims the right to Cantorian set theory, rejecting the intuitionist's effort to restrict set-theoretic inquiry, while at the same time preserving the normal domain V_ω, where constructivist studies with their own extrinsic virtues can still be carried out.[33] Thus, he takes the non-categoricity of ZF' as an advantage, not a disadvantage: "set theory as a *science* must . . . be developed in greatest generality" (Zermelo, 1930c, p. 45[427–428]). The italicized "science" is telling. Here, as in his earlier writings, it signifies his commitment to what he sees as productive mathematics. "The comparative investigation of individual *models*" (Zermelo, 1930c, p. 45[427–428]) is then one aspect of this productive project.

Under the banner of this generality, Zermelo also resists efforts to limit set theory to "the *lowest* infinitistic domain," to V_{κ_1}, for κ_1 the first inaccessible. An axiom to that effect would secure categoricity, but it would not "concern set theory *as such*"; it would "only characterize the special *model* chosen by the respective author" (Zermelo, 1930c, p. 45[427]). The better course is to acknowledge that the ordinals of V_{κ_1} constitute a boundary number greater than ω – namely, κ_1 – and that this uncountable boundary number itself exists as a set in a normal domain larger than V_{κ_1}.

> It is of course not possible to 'prove', that is, to deduce from the general ZF'-axioms, either its existence or non-existence, simply because, for instance, the boundary number ω, even though it exists in the 'Cantorian' domain [V_{κ_1}], does not exist in the 'finitistic' domain [V_ω], because, in other words, the question receives different answers in different 'models' of set theory, and is thus not decided merely by the axioms alone. (Zermelo, 1930c, p. 45[427])

So, in the interests of productive science, this and further boundary numbers should be posited in the background theory[34]:

---

33 We abuse notation by using V_ω for the hereditarily finite sets: it suggests the existence of ω, which, of course, is not present in that normal domain. We hope that this is understood, that the usage doesn't mislead, here and elsewhere, where V_κ is used for the normal domain whose boundary number is κ.

34 Zermelo also provides a somewhat inscrutable direct argument – what might be regarded as an intrinsic argument (cf. footnote 15) – for the existence of inaccessibles based on the assumption that "*every categorically determined domain can also be conceived of as a 'set'* . . . an element of a (suitably chosen) normal domain" (Zermelo, 1930c, p. 46 [429]). Given that the categorically determined domains are the V_κs, this comes to assuming that every V_κ is a set in a larger $V_{\kappa'}$.

> We must postulate the *existence of an unlimited sequence of boundary numbers* as a new axiom for the 'meta-theory of sets' . . . To the unlimited series of Cantorian ordinal numbers there corresponds a likewise unlimited . . . series of essentially different set-theoretic models in each of which the entire classical theory finds its expression. (Zermelo, 1930c, p. 47[429–431]).

The upshot of this line of thought is (1) an informal background theory that essentially comes to ZFC + I (where "I" asserts the existence of arbitrarily large inaccessibles), (2) the detailed development, in that background theory, of full models of the second-order theory ZF′, and (3) the heuristic, intuitive picture of the Iterative Conception.

To return, at last, to our leading question, has Zermelo's categoricity theorem (and the developments he bases on it) accomplished what he set out to accomplish? His explicit goal was to resolve the paradoxes, which he now dismisses in one characteristically combative sentence:

> The 'ultrafinite antinomies of set theory', to which scientific reactionaries . . . appeal in their fight against set theory with such eager passion, are only apparent 'contradictions', due only to a confusion between *set theory itself*, which is non-categorically determined by its axioms, and the individual *models* representing it: what in one model appears as 'ultrafinite . . .', is already a fully valid 'set' . . . in the next higher model and, in turn, serves itself as the bed-stone in the construction of the new domain. (Zermelo, 1930c, p. 47[429–431])

The class of all sets (or all ordinals) of one normal domain is just an ordinary set in the next – fine – but this doesn't solve the problem for the background theory: why is there no set of all sets (or all ordinals) there? Zermelo doesn't answer this question explicitly, but implicitly, he has a response of a piece with one offered by some observers to this day: there's no set of all sets because every set occurs in some normal domain, and no normal domain contains all sets.[35] Today, we might simply say there's no set of all sets because every set first appears at some stage of the iterative hierarchy, and there's no stage at which all sets are available to be collected. Of course, there's no contemporary consensus on the proper treatment of the paradoxes, but Zermelo's approach remains among the live options.

Still, in truth, it would be a grave mistake to count this approach to the paradoxes as the sole payoff to Zermelo's categoricity theorems. In that

---

[35] He says something very like this in Zermelo (1930a, p. 439): "Every normal domain is itself a 'set' in all higher domains, but there is no highest normal domain containing all normal domains as sets.'

retrospective report to the funding agency, Zermelo describes his goal more broadly than in "On boundary numbers" itself:

> I posed for myself the decisive preliminary question . . . How does a 'domain' of 'sets' and 'urelements' have to be constituted so that it satisfies the 'general' axioms of set theory? Is our axiom system 'categorical' or are there a multitude of essentially different 'set-theoretic' models? (Zermelo, 1930a, p. 437)

Giving answers to these questions is obviously a leading achievement of his Zermelo (1930c), but in Zermelo (1930a), Zermelo goes further. We noted earlier that the only defense of Foundation in Zermelo (1930c) is the observation that it "does not result in an essential restriction of the theory for the time being" (Zermelo, 1930c, p. 31[403]); now, in Zermelo (1930a), he explicitly acknowledges its indispensable role in the results of that paper[36]:

> In order to tackle [these goals] successfully, however, I first had to supplement the 'Zermelo-Fraenkel axiom system' by adding a further axiom, the 'foundation axiom' . . . By using the new axiom it was possible to carry out a decomposition into layers . . . of a 'normal domain' . . . and to answer the decisive main question in the 'isomorphism theorems'. (Zermelo, 1930a, p. 437)

The fact that Foundation enables the clarifying and fruitful breakdown of V into the V_αs constitutes a strong extrinsic argument in its favor, both as an axiom of ZF' and as an assumption of the background set theory.

Finally, beyond a viable candidate response to the paradoxes, beyond the clarification and insights arising from the theorem $V = \bigcup_{\alpha \in Ord} V_\alpha$ and its surroundings, beyond persuasive defense of the new axioms of Foundation and Inaccessibles, "On boundary numbers" introduced the Iterative Conception, whose mathematical fruitfulness for the future of set theory can hardly be overstated. In the end, then, Zermelo accomplished more than he set out to do – and ultimately more than he could have realized at the time – so this application of categoricity arguments must be counted as a resounding success.

4 Kreisel in "Informal Rigor and Incompleteness Proofs" (1967) and "Two Notes on the Foundations of Set Theory" (1969)

Kreisel's philosophical discussions of categoricity arguments in Kreisel (1969) and Kreisel (1967) have continued to influence contemporary thought on the

---

[36] Oddly, even in Zermelo (1930a), he doesn't acknowledge the decisive role of Replacement in his Zermelo (1930c). He remarks that it was Hausdorff's introduction of cofinality "that made possible a fruitful application of the new axiom" (Zermelo, 1930a, p. 435), omitting reference to von Neumann's use of Replacement for Transfinite Recursion, on which Zermelo (1930c) obviously draws (cf. Kanamori, 2010a, p. 432).

significance of such results, so we pause to ask what conclusions he intends to draw and to what extent he succeeds. (Since he presents no new mathematics, we dispense with our usual division into subsections.)

Looking back at "On boundary numbers," Zermelo notes in passing one consequence of its categoricity results:

> From this it already follows, among other things, that *Cantor's* ... conjecture ... does *not* depend on the choice of the model, but that it is decided (as true or as false) once and for all by means of our axiom system. (Zermelo, 1930a, p. 437)[37]

Understood as a theorem in Zermelo's background set theory, the claim is that CH has the same truth value in every normal domain,[38] but Kreisel reformulates it as a fact of second-order logic:

$$\text{ZFC}^2 \models CH \text{ or } \text{ZFC}^2 \models \neg CH.$$

What conclusion(s) does he draw from this?

Kreisel is often taken to have argued that this theorem of second-order logic shows that CH has a determinate truth value (even though, sadly, we haven't been able to figure out what that is).[39] In response, observers point out that if we're concerned that CH may not have a determinate truth value because we worry that the power set operation isn't fully determinate, then we are, or should be, just as concerned about the determinateness of the second-order quantifiers.[40] The resulting assessment is that Kreisel was wrong and no progress on CH has been made.

The surprise is that Kreisel is well aware of this problem, as he remarks in a long endnote:

> we still have the following *simple-minded puzzle*: is it not circular to use second order notions which involve the concept of set (or: subset) in axiomatizations of this concept? (Kreisel, 1969, p. 111, endnote 2)

This raises serious questions about what conclusions, if any, Kreisel is inclined to draw about the determinateness of CH – there's much to ponder in this

---

[37] Zermelo is actually referring to GCH, but here we keep the focus on CH. The claim is untenable, if not false, for GCH.

[38] Really, every normal domain with the same number of urelements. Our focus here is on "unit" normal domains, that is, normal domains with one urelement playing the role of ∅, so from now on, we ignore these niceties.

[39] See, for example, Button and Walsh (2018, p. 180).

[40] Weston was first to note this in print (see Weston, 1976). Button and Walsh (Button & Walsh, 2018, p. 158, note 17) list several others since. (Cf. Quine's assessment that higher-order logic is "set theory in sheep's clothing" [Quine, 1970, p. 66].) In contrast, Zermelo's set-theoretic proof that all normal domains agree on CH might as well be carried out in first-order ZFC.

endnote (see below) – but it's reasonable to assume that his central arguments appear, not there, but in the main text.

In fact, both articles are entirely explicit about his goal in appealing to the categoricity of ZFC[2]. Writing in the late 1960s, Kreisel was keen to isolate and articulate the significance of Cohen's recent independence results, as were many others in the set-theoretic and larger intellectual communities. (Kreisel also intended to improve "logical hygiene" [Kreisel, 1969, p. 109] by rebutting various popular misreadings.) Kreisel has a lot to say about this, some of it admittedly inconclusive, but he emphasizes one clear point in light of Zermelo's result, namely, the importance of

> *Distinctions* formulated in terms of higher order consequence. In contrast to the example of CH ..., Fraenkel's replacement axiom is not decided by Zermelo's Axioms (because [Zermelo's axioms plus Infinity are] satisfied by $[V_{\omega+\omega}]$ and Fraenkel's axiom is not); in particular it is independent of Zermelo's second order axioms while by Cohen's proof, CH is only independent of the *first order schema* (associated with the axioms) of Zermelo-Fraenkel. (Kreisel, 1967, pp. 150–151)

Returning to this point from Kreisel (1967) in Kreisel (1969), he puts it this way:

> The continuum hypothesis *CH* is (provably) *not* independent of the full (second order) version of ZERMELO's axioms; we know this much without knowing which way *CH* is decided; the example is not empty since, for instance, the replacement axiom *is* second-order independent. Needless to say, from the point of view of our present *knowledge* of the hierarchy of sets, it is of great interest to establish *what can and what cannot be decided* from the first order schemas or, as we might put it, *from our present analysis of the full axioms*. (Kreisel, 1969, p. 107)

In addition to its inherent importance, this demonstration of the distinction between first- and second-order independence also facilitates one of Kreisel's exercises in "logical hygiene": the popular analogy with the independence of the parallel postulate is misleading because the parallel postulate is independent of second-order geometry; the parallel postulate "corresponds to Fraenkel's axiom, not CH" (Kreisel, 1967, p. 151).[41]

But now, what about the determinateness of CH? In the endnote quoted above, he's considering the *standard argument* so often attributed to him, an argument to the conclusion – "subset of the reals" is determinate – from the premise – a second-order quantifier over the reals is determinate. If the familiar

---

[41] See also Kreisel (1969, p. 111, endnote 2).

reading of this paper were correct, we'd expect Kreisel to launch a direct defense against the circularity objection, but he doesn't. What he says is:

> Sure, it would be circular if one were looking for a *reduction*, a definition of this concept [of set (or: subset)] in, say, more elementary terms. (Kreisel, 1969, p. 111, endnote 2)

Well, yes, something like that is precisely what we're looking for in the standard argument: we're supposed to have confidence that the second-order quantifier is determinate – it's just logic, don't you see? – and that confidence is supposed to be transferred to the notion of subset.[42] A few lines later, he continues – "to suspect a *vicious* circle we should have to have independent reasons, such as the ambiguities mentioned at the beginning" (Kreisel, 1969, p. 111, endnote 2) of the paper, namely concerns about "the basic notion of set" (Kreisel, 1969, p. 94). Well, yes, again, the standard objection points out that someone who begins with worries about the concept of set won't be helped by the standard argument.

So it seems that such defense as Kreisel offers for the determinateness of CH isn't the standard argument, but a direct case against a few of the reasons one might have to worry about the notion of subset, and hence about CH, in the first place. The two reasons he considers are based on predicativism and finitism, respectively, and he argues that they're both "quite inconclusive" (Kreisel, 1969, p. 96). But surely there are other, more compelling grounds on which to doubt the determinacy of the notion of subset.

On this score, Kreisel himself doesn't seem entirely confident. Speaking just epistemologically, about our ability to determine the status of CH, he writes:

> There are a lot of subsets of ω, there are a lot of 1-1 mappings from ω to an initial segment of the ordinals; we certainly do not *know* . . . any listing of the subsets of ω by means of ordinals. So why should we expect to *know* the answer to this particular 'simple' matter? (Kreisel, 1969, p. 109)
> Doesn't one simply have an overwhelmingly strong impression that though we don't know how to decide CH, any decision would involve considerations of a quite *different character* from those which have led to existing axioms? (Kreisel, 1969, p. 108)

He observes that these new considerations needn't be " 'arbitrary' or even non-mathematical" (Kreisel, 1969, p. 108).

---

[42] For comparison, we might be suspicious of the semantic notion of first-order consequence and find that suspicion relieved by the discovery that it's equivalent with a syntactic one (Kreisel's own example).

He then moves from an epistemic worry that we don't know how to find the truth value of CH to a worry at issue in the standard argument, the worry that its truth value might be metaphysically indeterminate. The response he considers is based on what he calls "realism,"[43] which he criticizes on exactly this point earlier in the paper:

> there *is* or, at least, seems to be a genuine defect in the realist position generally and, in particular, in the unanalyzed use of the power set operation. (Kreisel, 1969, p. 97)

Given that he links the determinateness of power set with realism and that he takes this aspect of realism to be problematic, it's unlikely that vanquishing predicativism and finitism has left him immune from other worries about the notion of subset – and we've seen that he doesn't expect such worries to evaporate in the face of the standard argument.

To better understand Kreisel's attitude here, consider another criticism he lodges against realism, this one more methodological than epistemological or metaphysical:

> *By the second order decidability of CH, [realism] demonstratively does not provide a framework within which one can discuss the impression* [that considerations of a quite different character would be needed to settle it]. (Kreisel, 1969, p. 108, emphasis in the original)

It isn't immediately obvious why he thinks realism can't provide a framework for discussing the need for new methods, but there are clues. After dismissing the objections from predicativism and finitism, Kreisel tries out a realistic posture himself and examines "the cumulative type structure." From that perspective, he finds that "we have very good evidence for some of the axioms of infinity," for example, "when one recognizes that [a candidate] is a consequence of a second-order reflection principle then one has *found* good evidence" (Kreisel, 1969, pp. 98–99). Why is this evidence good? Because "the validity of the reflection principle becomes apparent on closer analysis of the hierarchy," because "in terms of *knowledge* of the unbounded hierarchy, reflection principles are quite evident" (Kreisel, 1969, pp. 98–99) – and he goes on to give an intrinsic argument based on the unattainability of V. So perhaps he thinks, as is not uncommon, that the only justificatory methods available to the realist are intrinsic, and given that he also thinks progress on CH will require methods of "a quite different character from those which have led to existing axioms" (Kreisel, 1969, p. 108), it would follow that realism hasn't

---

[43] He leaves many specifics of what he means by this far from univocal term to his reader's imagination.

the means to address the fundamental challenge posed by the phenomenon of its independence.

As an alternative to realism, he also considers what he calls "formalism."[44] Presumably a formalist eschews metaphysics, so isn't bound by the idea that only intrinsic considerations can be trusted to track the contours of some abstract subject matter. This leaves open the possibility of new methods, but unfortunately, "the formalist position does not normally *attempt* an analysis of the choice of system at all" (Kreisel, 1969, p. 108). Notice that this isn't a principled argument that a formalist couldn't take this on, just a complaint that his contemporary formalists don't – the possibility remains open of a version of formalism that does. Such a formalism might appeal, for example, to mathematical effectiveness in its justifications, to extrinsic justifications – following Zermelo.[45] In fact, Kreisel sees encouraging exploration of new methods as an "attempt to use [independence results] for some objectively significant purpose" (Kreisel, 1969, p. 110).[46]

Finally, one last observation from the fascinating endnote 2 of Kreisel (1969). We've seen that Kreisel regards the standard argument from the determinateness of second-order logic to that of CH as potentially viciously circular, but he also locates a benign circle in the vicinity. We might, he suggests, simply "use a concept in order to *state the facts* about it" (Kreisel, 1969, p. 111, endnote 2) and illuminate or develop a concept in this way. Consider, for example, the use of logical particles to advance an account of the satisfaction conditions for sentences containing the logical particles. He doesn't elaborate, but the idea must be that we better understand the subset operation and the second-order quantifier when we appreciate their interconnection in the case of CH.

---

[44] As with "realism" (see footnote 43), the particulars of this position, it's relation to other views of the same name, are left unexplored.

[45] The first author, predictably, thinks of the Arealism of her Maddy (2011) or the Enhanced If-thenism of her Maddy (2022). Kreisel comes close to this theme in a discussion of "pragmatism": he grants it a "superficial plausibility," but complains that it discourages "work on ... intuitive notions" (Kreisel, 1967, pp. 140–141). But this needn't be true; for example, we've already noted the immense heuristic value of Zermelo's Iterative Conception (cf., e.g., Maddy, 2011, p. 136). Kreisel also worries that a philosopher with such views will be left with nothing left to do, but the first author obviously disagrees.

[46] Kreisel (1969) closes with an implicit appeal for more such exploration:

> Here it must be admitted that, if CH, resp. ¬ CH is to be distinguished from other axioms of set theory by the *kind* of consideration needed to decide it, the crudity of current discussions is certainly not surprising. For though foundations have made striking progress in the precise analysis of *notions*, the analysis of reasons has been much less successful; and what *has* been done is little known. (Kreisel, 1969, p. 110)

In sum, then, Kreisel sees Zermelo's categoricity arguments as accomplishing at least two things. Since his overarching goal is to probe the significance of the independence results, his main focus is on the first of these: revealing that CH presents a new kind of independence – first-order but not second-order – which differentiates it from familiar cases like Replacement, large cardinals, or the parallel postulate. Along the way, in his analysis of the standard argument for the determinacy of CH, he observes that the categoricity results also provide a sort of elucidation or illumination of the concept of subset, by bringing out its interconnections with second-order quantification. As for the standard argument as intended, he doesn't appear to take the threat of circularity to be fully dispelled, but the determinateness of CH wasn't his target in the first place. At his actual goal – elucidating the independence phenomenon – he succeeds.

5 Parsons in "The Uniqueness of the Natural Numbers" (1990) and "Mathematical Induction" (2008)

5.1 What Does He Set Out to Accomplish?

In chapter 8 of his book, *Mathematical Thought and Its Objects* (Parsons, 2008) – especially "The problem of the uniqueness of the number structure" (section 48) and "Uniqueness and communication" (section 49) – Charles Parsons develops and refines the line of thought in his 1990 paper, "The uniqueness of the natural numbers" (Parsons, 1990). His topic isn't the uniqueness of individual natural numbers, like 3; as a structuralist, Parsons holds that various objects, perhaps various sets, for example, could play the role of 3 in the natural number structure. Rather, his concern is whether

> the natural numbers are at least determinate up to isomorphism: If two structures answer equally well to our conception of the sequence of natural numbers, they are isomorphic. (Parsons, 2008, section 48, p. 272)

A claim like this would be vacuous if there were no structure answering to our conception, but Parsons argues, like Dedekind before him, that there is at least one such (see below). As he understands it, "the initial, intuitive ground" (Parsons, 2008, section 48, p. 272) for concern is that our conception might be vague somehow, raising the possibility that it could be made precise in different ways.

The conception Parsons has in mind is given by the collection of rules stating that

$$N(0)$$

$$N(x) \rightarrow N(S(x))$$

$$S(0) \neq 0$$

$$\frac{S(x) = S(y)}{x = y}$$

$$P(x)$$
$$\vdots$$

$$\frac{P(0) \quad P(S(x)) \quad N(t)}{P(t)}$$

for any predicate P and term t.[47] An "inescapable vagueness" (Parsons, 2008, section 47, p. 270) arises because this characterization involves "induction as an inference that could be made with any well-defined predicate, without the prospect of specifying exactly what the range of such predicates is" (Parsons, 2008, section 48, pp. 272–273).[48] We call this understanding of a predicate variable "open-schematic."

The potential problem comes into sharper focus when we attend to Parsons's example of a structure that answers to our conception.[49] He starts from Hilbert (1926):

> Following Hilbert we begin by considering the 'syntax' of a 'language' with a single basic symbol '|' (stroke), whose well-formed expressions are just arbitrary strings containing just this symbol, i.e., |, ||, |||, ...(Parsons, 2008, section 28, p. 159)

On Parsons's account, we perceive these concrete tokens of strings. The string types he calls "quasi-concrete": they are abstract and acausal, but also typically intuited in the process of perceiving their tokens (assuming the perceiver enjoys the modest conceptual resources required).[50] Only typically, though, because concrete strings can also be imagined and their types intuited in that way.

But there are finite limits on the length and number of concrete inscriptions and even on the human capacity to imagine, so how do we get from here to

---

[47] See Parsons (2008, sections 31, 47).

[48] Parsons often discusses a purported threat of vagueness rooted in the existence of non-standard models, but ultimately concludes that it is "quite unconvincing" (Parsons, 2008, section 48, p. 279). We happily leave this aside, along with the difficult question of how a structure answering to a conception – for example, the Hilbertian stroke types described below – relates to a model of set-theoretic model theory. The "modelism" of Button and Walsh (2018) appears to solve this problem by fiat: "mathematical structures, as discussed informally by mathematicians, are best explicated by . . . a class of isomorphic models" (p. 38).

[49] See Parsons (2008, sections 28–29). Here and elsewhere, we use Parsons's own locution – "answers to our conception" – because we're unsure what would count as a fair paraphrase. More generally, our goal in this subsection is to describe Parsons's view, not to defend or endorse it.

[50] Again following Hilbert, Parsons (2008, section 28, p. 161) says that "intuition of a type [is] *founded* on perception of a token."

a potentially infinite sequence of types? How do we come to know that "each string of strokes *can* be extended by one more" (Parsons, 2008, section 29, p. 173)? Parsons's answer involves imagining "an arbitrary string of strokes" (Parsons, 2008, section 29, p. 173). As with Locke's idea of a general triangle – neither equilateral, nor isosceles, nor scalene –

> imagining an arbitrary string involves imagining a string of strokes without imagining its internal structure clearly enough to imagine a string of *n* strokes for some particular *n*. (Parsons, 2008, section 29, p. 173)

He compares this with imagining a "crowd at a baseball game without imagining a crowd consisting of 34,793 spectators" (Parsons, 2008, pp. 173–174). This will form Parsons's basis:

> To see the *possibility* of adding one more, it is only the general structure that we use, and not the specific fact that what we have before us was obtained by iterated additions of one more. (Parsons, 2008, p. 175)

Building on this idea of a general structure, Parsons offers two ways of justifying the claim that one more can always be added – involving our perception of figure/ground or of temporal succession[51] – with the upshot that "our insight into [the necessity that every string can be extended] is insight into experienced space and time" (Parsons, 2008, p. 178). The Kantian echo is obvious, but notice that the faculties involved in Parsons's Hilbertian intuitive picture[52] (as we'll call it) aren't aspects of transcendental psychology or philosophical constructs like "rational intuition"[53] but aspects of ordinary human perception and cognition.

Perhaps it's unsurprising that a concept instantiated by such a structure, based in human imagination, would be considered potentially vague in one troublesome sense or other. Like the imagined baseball crowd, our imaginings are indeterminate in an indefinite range of aspects. (Try imagining a perfect summer day or the Mona Lisa, then ask yourself how many questions you can

---

[51] The first is derived from our perceptual ability to "shift [our] attention so that what was previously ground is now figure" (Parsons, 2008, section 29, p. 177) and the other (developing Brouwer's "temporal two-ity") is derived from the fact that "we experience the world as temporal, and have the conviction that we can continue into the proximate future, in which the immediate past is retained" (Parsons, 2008, section 29, p. 177). Whatever Parsons may have intended, he offers no reason to suppose these are anything other than ordinary cognitive mechanisms studied in empirical psychology.

[52] We call this an "intuitive picture" rather than a "concept" or "structure" to indicate that it's not an epistemic or metaphysical but a psychological phenomenon.

[53] Parsons does discuss a form of rational intuition in chapter 9 of Parsons (2008), but in explicit contrast to the intuition of chapter 5, the notion engaged here. (Recall footnote 51.)

honestly answer about the features of the resulting "image.") As for Parsons's imagined Hilbertian series of strings of strokes, "what if the picture began to flicker in the far distance?" (Wittgenstein, *Remarks on the foundations of mathematics* [Wittgenstein, 1978, V.10, p. 268]).

What Parsons wants is assurance that nothing like this happens, that our concept of natural number specifies a unique and determinate structure. Following Michael Dummett, he poses the problem in terms of communication: how can I be sure that your numbers are like mine?[54] Maybe I'm working with one precification of our shared vague concept and you're working with another. Or, as Parsons prefers to pose the question, consider two speakers of a first-order language of arithmetic, Kurt and Michael, both of whom embrace the Peano axioms, and then, "we might ask how one could come to know that his 'numbers' are isomorphic to the other's" (Parsons, 2008, section 49, p. 283). This is the question Parsons hopes to answer by appealing to a categoricity argument. Exactly how a positive answer would bear on the original question of the determinateness of our concept is a topic for Section 5.3.[55]

5.2 What Does He Actually Do (or Can Be Done)?

Given this goal, one's first thought is Dedekind's theorem (Section 2.2), and that's precisely where Parsons's discussion begins.[56] The first version of Dedekind's result, Theorem 1, is a weakly internal argument (the description of simply finite systems is used not mentioned[57]) based on what might as well be a weak first-order set theory. Parsons would presumably agree to the conclusion Dedekind draws – that the structure of the natural numbers can be described without appeal to temporal or geometric intuition – though his Hilbertian instance of that structure depends on both perceptual

---

[54] The only argument for this move – from a question about the determinateness of a structure to a question about communication – that we could find in the two Dummett essays that Parsons cites (Dummett, 1963, 1967) appears in the course of his evaluation of a version of Platonism, in particular, one based on an analogy between intuition of abstract structures and ordinary perception. If our intuition of the structure of natural numbers couldn't be communicated, "this would reduce the intuitive observation of abstract structures to something private and incommunicable – the analog not of observation of the physical world in the normal sense, but of the experience of sense data as conceived by those philosophers who hold these to be private and incommunicable" (Dummett, 1967, p. 210). But Parsons's concern isn't with Platonism, much less this particular variety thereof; he's posed his challenge in terms of concepts – for example, is your understanding of the concept of natural number the same as mine? – not in terms of reference, as some do – are you talking about the same numbers as I am? (See, e.g., the "objects-modelism" of Button & Walsh, 2018, pp. 144–145.) This focus on concepts rather than ontology explains the focus on actual human faculties noted above.

[55] Recall footnote 54.

[56] See Parsons (2008, sections 10–11).

[57] Recall footnote 10.

and imaginative intuitions.[58] Still, to Parsons's mind, the role of set theory is problematic.

Early on in Parsons (2008), he writes that 'we do not think of elementary number theory as involving commitment to properties, sets, classes, or Fregean concepts" (Parsons, 2008, section 5, p. 20), a sentiment repeated in the later discussion of uniqueness:

> It is a commonplace in the foundations of mathematics that the idea of natural number is more elementary than that of set. (Parsons, 2008, section 48, p. 274)

Presumably, this means that Kurt could believe the Peano axioms while innocent of the concept of set, so this version of Dedekind's argument is of no use to him.[59] What Parsons wants, then, is a categoricity theorem for arithmetic that relies on no resources beyond what's available to Kurt himself, no resources beyond those of number theory itself – what might be called a *pure* categoricity argument.[60]

The external version of Dedekind's result, Theorem 2, also depends on set theory and thus faces the same impurity objection that Parsons raises to Theorem 1. Still, the introduction of second-order semantics reminds us that

$$N \models \mathrm{PA}^2 \wedge N' \models \mathrm{PA}^2 \rightarrow N \cong N'$$

is, in fact, a truth of second-order logic alone. In this form, it's obviously subject to a number-theoretic version of the challenge raised in Section 4, the one Kreisel hasn't fully overcome: if you're worried about the determinateness of the range of predicates allowed in the open-schematic induction axiom, as Parsons is, then you're also nervous about the determinateness of second-order quantification. More in line with Parsons's thinking,[61] the second-order logical truth can be recast without semantics, as a weakly internal theorem in syntactic second-order logic. Let $\mathrm{PA}^2(X, Y, Z)$ be the second-order Peano axioms formulated for a unary predicate, a unary function symbol, and a constant, and let

---

[58] Both Dedekind and Parsons appeal to roughly psychological instantiations of their structures – Dedekind's thoughts of thoughts of thoughts (Dedekind, 1888, section 66) and Parsons's Hilbertian perceived and imagined strokes – to establish that their structural descriptions aren't vacuous. They differ when Dedekind insists on abstracting (creating) the numbers themselves; Parsons is content to rest with the structure.

[59] In response, it might be argued that the concept of finite set is essentially bound up with the concept of natural number, so that Kurt necessarily believes some set theory along with his assumptions about numbers.

[60] We allude here to related themes of purity of method in the philosophy of mathematics. For an overview, see, for example, Detlefsen and Arana (2011).

[61] See Parsons (2008, pp. 45–46).

ISO$((X, Y, Z), (X', Y', Z'))$ be the second-order sentence claiming that there's an isomorphism between (X, Y, Z) and (X', Y', Z'). Then[62]

Theorem 6 $\vdash_2 \forall N_1, S_1, 0_1, N_2, S_2, 0_2((PA^2(N_1, S_1, 0_1) \land PA^2(N_2, S_2, 0_2)) \rightarrow$ ISO$((N_1, S_1, 0_1), (N_2, S_2, 0_2)))$.

The proof involves only Π_1^1-comprehension, but Parsons echoes the same concern about even that much: there's "a question whether the second-order quantifiers . . . can have a definite sense" (Parsons, 2008, section 47, p. 270). In particular, even Π_1^1-comprehension is committed to a well-determined range of predicates of natural numbers.[63]

So, given Kurt's epistemic situation, Parsons wants a pure theorem. Given his objections to second-order logic, either semantic or syntactic, it must also be first-order. Finally, in light of these two desiderata, any appeal to semantic notions is problematic, so such an argument must be weakly internal. (Notice that the preference for internalness isn't for its own sake but as a means toward achieving the other two desiderata.) To sum up: the goal is a pure weakly internal argument – let's call this *strongly internal* or just *internal*[64] – that's also first-order. This is the bar Parsons sets himself.

Before asking how Parsons undertakes to do this and how his sketch can be developed, we pause to note some fundamental differences between Dedekind's project and Parsons's – in the role of a background metaphysics and in motivation. Both begin with a kind of pre-theoretic metaphysics: Dedekind his sets and Parsons his structures. (We haven't and won't attempt to pinpoint their precise ontological status – realistic, idealistic, or otherwise.) Dedekind begins by codifying a few relevant features of his sets and using those assumptions to study something else (the concept of natural number). In contrast, Parsons never produces an explicit theory of structures – they remain pre-theoretic, doing no explicit mathematical work – but they are, nevertheless, the ultimate object of study (in particular, the natural number structure). On motivation, Dedekind has no doubts about the determinateness of his concept

---

[62] $\vdash_2$ is derivability in the usual axiom system of second-order logic: first-order axioms, introduction and elimination rules for the second-order quantifiers, plus all instances of comprehension and choice (see, e.g., Shapiro (1991, pp. 66–67) and Button and Walsh (2018, p. 34).) Button and Walsh (2018, pp. 240–241) recommend that Parsons content himself with this result. The text indicates why Parsons rules this out.

[63] Presumably he'd raise an analogous objection to the set-quantifiers in the weak set-theoretic versions of Dedekind's argument, even apart from the impurity problem.

[64] For the record, the term "internal categoricity" was first used in Walmsley (2002). After Parsons (1990), the idea occurred more or less explicitly throughout the 1990s and beyond, for example, in Shapiro (1991), Lavine (1994), McGee (1997), and Lavine (1999), as well as Väänänen and Wang (2015) and Väänänen (2021).

of natural number, he's only interested in what it takes to characterize it, while for Parsons, the whole inquiry arises from his worry that the concept might be vague or otherwise indeterminate. So, despite the fact that both are focused on the concept of natural number, despite the fact that Parsons appropriates the mathematical core of Dedekind's theorem, their philosophical perspectives and their goals are quite different.

So, how does Parsons hope to pull this off; how is Kurt to prove that his numbers are isomorphic to Michael's using only first-order number-theoretic tools? We know the first-order Peano axioms aren't enough, but we've ruled out a move to second-order. Perhaps ironically, Parsons hopes to locate a happy medium between too weak and too strong by exploiting the open-schematic character of the induction rule in his characterization of the concept of natural number, the very feature that led to his worry over vagueness in the first place.

The idea is that open-schematic induction takes us beyond the usual first-order axiom, which allows only formulas from a fixed vocabulary, but not far enough to generate a second-order quantifier:

> In . . . referring to arbitrary predicates, the statement of the rule makes no assumption about what counts as a predicate. . . . The rule is not a generalization over a given domain of entities and could not be, because it is not determined what predicates will or can be constructed and understood. . . . Replacing the rule by an axiom, that is, a single statement expressed by quantification over sets . . . is not suitable for the explanation of the number concept by rules that we have been engaged in. (Parsons, 2008, section 47, pp. 269–270)
>
> This understanding of induction implies that the applicability of the rule is not limited to predicates defined in some particular first-order language such as that of first-order arithmetic. But we must not take it as implying the unavoidability or even the legitimacy of second-order logic . . . second-order logic is not forced on us. (Parsons, 2008, section 47, p. 270)

Not all observers agree on this last point. For example, see Shapiro – "the effect is the same as allowing only initial universal quantifiers over second-order variables" (Shapiro, 1991, p. 246) – or Field – "so we have an analog, in the schematic first-order case, of assertions of Π^1_1 second-order sentences" (Field, 2001, p. 354) – or Button and Walsh – "this is to fall back on (a syntactic fragment of) full second-order logic . . . our grasp on the idea of *totally* open-ended induction is exactly as precarious as our grasp on *full* second-order quantification" (Button & Walsh, 2018, pp. 240, 163).

This is a debate we hope not to engage. If these observers are wrong and open-schematic induction isn't just a re-description of a weak form of second-order logic, then it's hard to see how a precise mathematical treatment could be given; it would require a formal account of "any well-defined predicate" that avoids "specifying exactly what the range of such predicates is" (Parsons, 2008, section 48, pp. 272–273). We prefer a different route in pursuit of Parsons's goal: investigating what unproblematically first-order resources Kurt would need to argue for the desired isomorphism.

So, suppose Kurt speaks of his numbers, his successor function, and his first number, Michael speaks of his, and they believe many of the same arithmetic truths. How can Kurt be sure they're talking about the same structure? To pose the question more precisely, let N_1 and N_2 be unary predicate symbols, S_1 and S_2 unary function symbols, and 0_1 and 0_2 constant symbols.[65] Then let T_1 be the first-order Peano axioms for $(N_1, 0_1, S_1)$ with induction formulated as a schema in the vocabulary $\{N_1, 0_1, S_1\} \cup \{N_2, 0_2, S_2\}$, that is,

$$(\psi(0_1, \vec{y}) \wedge \forall x((N_1(x) \wedge \psi(x, \vec{y})) \rightarrow \psi(S_1(x), \vec{y}))) \rightarrow \\ \forall x(N_1(x) \rightarrow \psi(x, \vec{y})), \tag{5.1}$$

where $\psi(x, \vec{y})$ is any first-order formula in the vocabulary $\{N_1, 0_1, S_1\} \cup \{N_2, 0_2, S_2\}$. Let T_2 be the corresponding theory for $(N_2, 0_2, S_2)$.

Kurt's native language is built on the vocabulary $\{N_1, S_1, 0_1\}$, but his theory of natural numbers is T_1, which extends his schematic induction principle to allow vocabulary from Michael's language, built on $\{N_2, S_2, 0_2\}$. This means that the formula ψ in the induction schema of T_1 can include vocabulary beyond the native language of $(N_1, 0_1, S_1)$ into the language of $(N_2, S_2, 0_2)$ and that its quantifiers range beyond N_1 to include N_2. This is stronger than what we ordinarily mean by first-order Peano arithmetic; by including more instances of induction, it moves in the direction of second-order PA. (Obviously, this is also true of Michael, mutatis mutandis.) In addition, Kurt's understanding of Michael entails that he recognizes T_2 as holding in that added ontology, so his working theory includes $T_1 \cup T_2$.

With this added strength, Kurt, arguing in T_1, can use his induction schema to prove first-order statements about relationships between the two vocabularies. This raises the possibility that Kurt's $T_1 \cup T_2$ might be enough to produce the isomorphism he's hoping for, an isomorphism ϕ between $(N_1, S_1, 0_1)$ and $(N_2, S_2, 0_2)$.[66] So, is $T_1 \cup T_2$ enough to prove categoricity? As it happens, the answer is no.[67]

---

[65] As it happens, $+$ and $\cdot$ are definable from 0 and S in second-order PA, but not in first-order PA, so it would make more sense to include them here. We remain faithful to Parsons's presentation for now, but switch to including $+$ and $\cdot$ below, when the question is how to replicate something like second-order internal categoricity in a first-order setting.

[66] In embryonic form, this idea is due to Corcoran (1980).

[67] Button and Walsh make a similar observation in their Proposition 10.4 (Button & Walsh, 2018, section 10.C).

Remark 1 $T_1 \cup T_2$ *cannot produce such a ϕ.*

Proof: Our goal is to construct a model M' of $T_1 \cup T_2$ such that struc-
tures $(N_1^{M'}, 0_1^{M'}, S_1^{M'})$ and $(N_2^{M'}, 0_2^{M'}, S_2^{M'})$ are non-isomorphic – so that Parsons's
desired ϕ cannot exist. First, let M be a model of the vocabulary of $T_1 \cup T_2$ such
that M is the disjoint sum of two copies of the standard model $(\mathbb{N}, 0, S)$. Thus
$(N_1^M, 0_1^M, S_1^M) \cong (\mathbb{N}, 0, S)$ and $(N_2^M, 0_2^M, S_2^M) \cong (\mathbb{N}, 0, S)$. Then let $(\mathbb{N}^*, 0^*, S^*)$ be
a countable non-standard model elementarily equivalent to (but again disjoint
from) $(\mathbb{N}, 0, S)$ and let M' be the disjoint sum of $(\mathbb{N}, 0, S)$ and $(\mathbb{N}^*, 0^*, S^*)$, mak-
ing it a model of the vocabulary of $T_1 \cup T_2$. A simple Ehrenfeucht–Fraïssé
game argument, as in Feferman (1972), shows that $M \equiv M'$. Since $(\mathbb{N}, 0, S)$
satisfies even the second-order Induction Axiom, M certainly satisfies T_1.
Respectively, M satisfies T_2. Thus $M \models T_1 \cup T_2$ and then also $M' \models T_1 \cup T_2$.
But $(N_1^{M'}, 0_1^{M'}, S_1^{M'})$ and $(N_2^{M'}, 0_2^{M'}, S_2^{M'})$ are non-isomorphic, as the former is
standard and the latter is non-standard.   □

Though this argument demonstrates that $T_1 \cup T_2$ isn't enough to generate the
desired ϕ, it also gives a hint of what more is needed. The two non-isomorphic
countable models in the proof are n-equivalent for all n. For countable structures, isomorphism is equivalent to the existence of a winning strategy for the
so-called isomorphism player in the Ehrenfeucht–Fraïssé game of length ω. So
the point of the above counter-example is that the models imitate being isomorphic, in the sense that the isomorphism player has a winning strategy, up
to n moves of the Ehrenfeucht–Fraïssé game, for every n separately, but if infi-
nitely many moves are allowed, the non-isomorphism player has a winning
strategy. The finite strategies corresponding to different finite lengths of the
game do not cohere. We need a global principle that knits the different finite
pieces together, essentially a winning strategy in the infinite game. The strength
gained by replacing the usual induction schemas in two copies of first-order PA
with the more generous induction principles of T_1 and T_2 isn't enough, but there
are enhancements that are up to the task.

Parsons's preferred enhancement is primitive recursion.[68] In particular, he
introduces his ϕ by recursion on N_1:

$$\begin{cases} \phi(0_1) = 0_2 \\ \phi(S_1(x)) = S_2(\phi(x)). \end{cases}$$

He then reprises Dedekind's proof from Section 2.2; to show ϕ is one-to-one,
he applies N_1-induction to $\forall m(\phi(n) = \phi(m) \rightarrow n = m)$; to show ϕ is onto

---

[68] See Parsons (2008, section 49, p. 281): "in keeping with Skolem's recursive arithmetic, we can
introduce by primitive recursion a functor."

N_2, he applies N_2-induction to $\exists m(\phi(m) = n)$. (He notes that both instances of induction are first-order.) Clearly this ϕ would be the required isomorphism.

Unfortunately, Parsons's brief presentation doesn't extend beyond his gesture toward "Skolem's recursive arithmetic," so the challenge is to formulate a first-order internal theorem that captures the required recursion. The standard method involves some version of Π_1^1-comprehension and a second-order induction axiom – and, as we know, Parsons's vision requires that second-order logic, however weak, be abandoned altogether. What he wants is a first-order extension of $T_1 \cup T_2$ that's capable of generating the required isomorphism between Kurt's numbers and Michael's. Precisely what it takes to do this is a difficult technical question because of the way ϕ crosses from one vocabulary to another – existing results in reverse mathematics deal with one version of arithmetic at a time. We explore what's known of the mathematical situation, drawing on and extending the second author's work in Väänänen and Wang (2015) (jointly with Wang) and Väänänen (2021). First-order formulations introduce some non-trivial complications, so we begin with the second-order case as a warm up.

Consider, then, a second-order theory T_1^2 in the vocabulary $\{R_1, \ldots, R_n\}$, where R_i is r_i-ary for $1 \leq i \leq n$.[69] Suppose $\{R_1', \ldots, R_n'\}$ are new relation symbols such that the arity of R_i' is r_i for $1 \leq i \leq n$, and T_2^2 is the theory T_1^2 with every occurrence of R_i replaced by R_i', $1 \leq i \leq n$. Let F be a new unary function symbol, U and U' be new unary predicate symbols, and $\mathrm{ISO}(F, U, U')$ the first-order formula which says that F is a bijection between U and U' such that $R_i(a_1, \ldots, a_{r_i}) \leftrightarrow R_i'(F(a_1), \ldots, F(a_{r_i}))$ for all $a_1, \ldots, a_n \in U$ and all i with $1 \leq i \leq n$. If ϕ is any second-order formula, we let $\phi^{(U)}$ denote the formula obtained from ϕ by relativizing all first- and second-order quantifiers to U. Finally, for any theory T, $T^{(U)}$ denotes $\{\phi^{(U)} : \phi \in T\}$. We then formally define:

Definition 3 *The second order theory T_1^2 is internally categorical if*

$$T_1^{2(U)} \cup T_2^{2(U')} \vdash_2 \exists F\, \mathrm{ISO}(F, U, U'), \tag{5.2}$$

where $T_1^{2(U)} \cup T_2^{2(U')}$ appears on the left side of the turnstile – as opposed to the right side, which may seem more natural for categoricity claims – simply to allow for infinite theories.

Intuitively, T_1^2 stipulates some axioms for a relational structure with the relations $\{R_1, \ldots, R_n\}$, and it does so without semantic notions. Similarly, T_2^2

---

[69] We assume for simplicity that the vocabulary is relational and finite. Neither constraint is essential. When we refer to constants, such as 0 in PA^2, we think of them here as unary relations which are singletons.

stipulates the same axioms for the relational structure with $\{R'_1, \ldots, R'_n\}$ as the relations. The sentence $\mathrm{ISO}(F, U, U')$ says that F is an isomorphism between the two relational structures when their domains are restricted to U and U', respectively. The categoricity of T_1^2 is obviously equivalent to the statement that the second-order sentence $\exists F\, \mathrm{ISO}(F, U, U')$ is true in any full model of $T_1^{2(U)} \cup T_2^{2(U')}$. But (5.2) says that the categoricity of T_1^2 is not just a set-theoretical fact but is, in fact, provable in second-order logic. Semantically, this means that every Henkin model of $T_1^{2(U)} \cup T_2^{2(U')}$ satisfies $\exists F\, \mathrm{ISO}(F, U, U')$. In other words, if a Henkin model recognizes two models of T_1^2, it also recognizes an isomorphism between those two models.

Notice, then, that internal categoricity is more general than our familiar notion of categoricity:

Theorem 7 *Suppose T_1^2 is internally categorical. Then T_1^2 is categorical, that is, if $M \models T_1^2$ and $M' \models T_1^2$, where M and M' are full models, then $M \cong M'$.*

Proof: W.l.o.g., suppose the domains of M and M', which we denote also with M and M', are disjoint. Let M^* be the unique model with $M \cup M'$ as domain, $U^{M^*} = M$, $U'^{M^*} = M'$, $R_i^{M^*} = R_i^M$, and $R'^{M^*}_i = R_i^{M'}$ for $1 \leq i \leq n$. Clearly, $M^* \models T_1^{2(U)} \cup T_2^{2(U')}$. Hence by internal categoricity,

$$(U^{M^*}, R_1^{M^*}, \ldots, R_n^{M^*}) \cong (U'^{M^*}, R'^{M^*}_1, \ldots, R'^{M^*}_n).$$

Now $M \cong M'$ follows. $\qquad\qquad\square$

In particular, when T_1^2 is PA^2, we have

Theorem 8 (e.g., Hellman, 1989) *PA^2 is internally categorical.*

Dedekind's original result follows immediately:

Corollary 1 (Dedekind) *PA^2 is categorical.*

This brings the story of internal categoricity for second-order theories full circle.

Despite the purity of Theorem 8, its second-order character obviously rules it out for Parsons's purposes, so let's now see to what extent this general approach can be adapted to a first-order context. For various reasons that aren't directly relevant here,[70] it's not easy to define first-order internal categoricity for general theories T. Instead, since our particular interest is in

---

[70] For theories with first-order schemas arising from second-order Π_1^1-axioms, it's clear how to define internal categoricity, but for first-order theories in general the question is open.

theories of arithmetic, we explore possibilities for a first-order analog to Definition 3 that's designed specifically for the case of the Peano axioms. To that end, suppose the vocabulary of PA is $\{+, \cdot, 0, 1\}$.[71] Let N_1 and N_2 be unary predicate symbols, $+_1$ and $+_2$, $\cdot_1$ and $\cdot_2$ binary function symbols, and 0_1 and 0_2, 1_1 and 1_2 constant symbols. Then let $PA_1(N_1)$ be the first-order theory PA written in the vocabulary $\{+_1, \cdot_1, 0_1, 1_1\}$, with the functions $+_1, \cdot_1$ mapping $N_1 \times N_1$ to N_1, the constants $0_1, 1_1$ in N_1, but with adjustments reminiscent of T_1: the Induction Schema allows formulas from the larger vocabulary $\{+, \cdot, 0, 1\} \cup \{+_1, \cdot_1, 0_1, 1_1\} \cup \{+_2, \cdot_2, 0_2, 1_2\}$ and (first-order) quantifiers range over the whole domain, including $N_1 \cup N_2$. Likewise $PA_2(N_2)$.

The first, obvious obstacle to a first-order project is that the basic claim of categoricity – "there's an isomorphism between N_1 and N_2" – can't be formulated in our first-order language. It might be possible, however, to devise a first-order formula, $\phi(x, y)$, that determines a functional relation of the desired form. Devising an appropriate ϕ involves coding. Let $\psi(x, u, v)$ say that x, using $+$ and $\cdot$, codes an initial segment I_1 of N_1 ending with u, an initial segment I_2 of N_2 ending with v, and a function $f: I_1 \rightarrow I_2$ such that $f(0_1) = 0_2$, $f(z +_1 1_1) = f(z) +_2 1_2$ for all $z \in I_1$ preceding u in I_1, and $f(u) = v$. Then let $\phi(u, v)$ be $\exists x \psi(x, u, v)$. Saying that ϕ is an isomorphism is straightforward: let $ISO_\phi(N_1, N_2)$ be the first-order formula which says that ϕ is a bijection between N_1 and N_2, and for all $x, y \in N_1$:

$$
\begin{aligned}
&F(0_1) = 0_2 \wedge \\
&F(1_1) = 1_2 \wedge \\
&F(x +_1 y) = F(x) +_2 F(y) \wedge \\
&F(x \cdot_1 y) = F(x) \cdot_2 F(y),
\end{aligned}
\tag{5.3}
$$

where $F(x)$ abbreviates the unique $y \in N_2$ such that $\phi(x, y)$.

With this machinery in place, a version of categoricity can be proved from a collection of first-order arithmetic assumptions. With ϕ as above:

Theorem 9 (Väänänen, 2021)   *First-order PA is* internally categorical *in the sense that*

$$
PA \cup PA_1(N_1) \cup PA_2(N_2) \vdash ISO_\phi(N_1, N_2).
\tag{5.4}
$$

Proof: By induction on $+_1$, we show that F is a function $N_1 \rightarrow N_2$ and that it satisfies the conditions (5.3). We then use induction on $+_2$ to prove that F is onto. These proofs exploit the fact that induction holds for first-order formulas

---

[71]   Recall footnote 65.

that have any of the symbols $+, \cdot, 0, 1, +_1, \cdot_1, 0_1, 1_1, +_2, \cdot_2, 0_2, 1_2$. Induction on $+$ is used to establish the necessary properties of the coding.   □

Intuitively speaking, from the perspective of PA, the rest of the left-hand side of the turnstile in (5.4) tells us that there are two models $(N_1, +_1, \cdot_1, 0_1, 1_1)$ and $(N_2, +_2, \cdot_2, 0_2, 1_2)$ with $N_1, N_2 \subseteq N$, both of which satisfy the axioms of first-order PA. From these assumptions, Theorem 9 tells us that ϕ is an isomorphism between them. As with second-order internal categoricity (Theorem 8), this is true even if the model of PA we're working in is non-standard or uncountable. It's easy to see that the internal categoricity (and thereby the categoricity) of PA^2 follows from the internal categoricity of the first-order PA in the sense of Theorem 9.

Though it comes close, the sense of "internal categoricity" in Theorem 9 doesn't look quite like that of Definition 3, largely because of that extra PA on the left-hand side. But note that, in Definition 3, the comprehension axioms are built into $\vdash_2$. This is where the hidden power of second-order comprehension comes into dramatic focus: it's simply assumed that the range of the second-order quantifier includes an item for every formula in the combined vocabularies of $T_1^{2(U)} \cup T_2^{2(U)}$; this is what generates the required bijection, the required link between the two models. In the first-order case, where no such implicit background is in place, the extra PA is required to play this role. (And, for the record, Dedekind's weak set theory does the same in his Theorem 1.)

Another option is to consider two copies of PA with the same domain: PA_1^* says that the axioms of first-order PA hold of $+_1, \cdot_1, 0_1, 1_1$, PA_2^* says the same for $+_2, \cdot_2, 0_2, 1_2$, where both allow induction for first-order formulas in the joint vocabulary $\{+_1, \cdot_1, 0_1, 1_1\} \cup \{+_2, \cdot_2, 0_2, 1_2\}$. If AUT_ϕ says that ϕ defines a permutation of the domain and that it satisfies the preservation clauses in the definition of $ISO_\phi(N_1, N_2)$, then we get this result:

Theorem 10 (Väänänen, 2019, 2021)   *First-order Peano arithmetic PA is* internally categorical *in the sense that*

$$PA_1^* \cup PA_2^* \vdash AUT_\phi. \tag{5.5}$$

This mimics Definition 3 more closely: there's no extra PA overseeing the two copies PA_1^* and PA_2^*. Still, the assumption that the two copies have the same domain (which, incidentally, needn't be countable) makes Theorem 10 less compelling than Theorem 9. Intuitively speaking, we're trying to establish that two models of first-order arithmetic are isomorphic, and (knowing that this is impossible without some extra assumption) we make the task easier by assuming that we are "half way there" in the sense that at least the two models have the same domain.

5.3 Does He (or Can He) Accomplish What He Set Out to Do?

Does any of this help Kurt determine whether or not Michael's numbers are isomorphic to his own? In Theorem 9, he begins from PA – not $PA_1(N_1)$, his own idiosyncratic version – and views both $PA_1(N_1)$ and Michael's version from that broader point of view. It's hard to see how this could honestly be described as Kurt proving, exclusively from his own perspective, that his numbers are isomorphic to Michael's.[72] Theorem 10 would return Kurt to his own perspective, but he would need to know in advance that Michael is talking about the same things he is – though perhaps getting some of their properties and relations wrong – and it's hard to see what grounds he could have for this belief.[73] So far, at least, the mathematics of internal categoricity hasn't delivered a first-order result that Kurt can deploy, hasn't shown that Parsons can avoid an appeal to second-order logic. This obviously isn't conclusive, but the challenge hasn't yet been met.

On the philosophical aspects of Parsons's effort, consider again the question he set out to answer: is our shared concept of natural number univocal, or can "two [different] structures answer equally well to our conception of the sequence of natural numbers" (Parsons, 2008, section 48, p. 272)? As we've seen, he then characterizes our shared concept in terms of a set of rules that include the open-schematic version of mathematical induction and offers his Hilbertian intuitive picture of ever-increasing strings of strokes as an example of a structure that answers to it. As noted earlier, Parsons's account of this picture calls on ordinary human psychology – perception of figure/ground or temporal succession, "insight into experienced space and time" (Parsons, 2008, section 29, p. 178) – so the number concept it answers to would seem to be one shared by adult humans beyond the developmental levels of understanding counting[74] and realizing there's no largest number.[75] It's the shared understanding of $1, 2, 3, \ldots$ that we use every day, in contexts both mundane and theoretical.

Now consider some recent psychological findings of Josephine Relaford-Doyle and Rafael Núñez at UCSD (Relaford-Doyle & Núñez, 2017, 2018, 2021). The experimental subjects were college students, one group drawn from

---

[72] There's also the murkier question of whether Kurt – whose thinking, we assume, is relentlessly first-order – could replicate the line of thought that came before Theorem 9. It might be argued that understanding the significance of ϕ depends on seeing it as a first-order replacement for the second-order $\exists f$, which would be reason to doubt that a relentlessly first-order Kurt would see its significance, let alone be inspired to think it up (cf. Kreisel, 1967, p. 148). For that matter, how would a relentlessly first-order Kurt pose the question of categoricity to himself in the first place?

[73] Obviously, the concern of the previous footnote arises here as well.

[74] Around age 4. See Spelke (2000).

[75] Around age 6. See Chu, Cheung, Schneider, Sullivan, and Barner (2020).

the general population without training in mathematics and another from mathematics majors with at least a B- in a course on proof techniques that included mathematical induction. Subjects were shown a visual argument that the sum of the first n odd numbers is n^2:

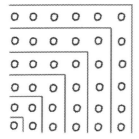

Here, the first odd number, 1, is represented by one dot in the lower, left-hand corner: $1 = 1^2$. The second odd number, 3, is represented by adding three dots so as to form a 2×2 square: $(1 + 3 = 2^2)$. Then, 5 is represented by adding five dots in the same way so as to form a 3×3 square: $1 + 3 + 5 = 3^2$. And so on. The recursive character of the construction is clear; an induction to all natural numbers is implicit.[76]

   Or so it seems. The experimenters focused on subjects who demonstrated that they understood the statement (the sum of the first n odd numbers is n^2) and were willing to generalize to nearby numbers (having gone through the argument for the first five odd numbers, they believed it would hold for seven or eight). These subjects were then asked a striking question: might there be a large number for which the statement fails? The answer seems obvious – surely not! – but that was the reaction of only a third of the mathematically trained respondents and fewer than 10% of the rest; nearly 40% of the untrained subjects and 10% of the trained respondents saw the existence of such a counterexample as plausible. The thought was that "larger numbers could be . . . outliers" or "when it gets to really high numbers . . . it's possible that . . . maybe it gets kind of fuzzy. Because at extremes things tend not to work as they do normally" or perhaps most tellingly, "it's too hard to draw a million dots" (Relaford-Doyle & Núñez, 2021, p. 14). One subject, a math and computer science major in the mathematically trained group, made explicit reference to computational limitations: "Large numbers have problems. In computer science . . . even if it works on small, medium, most numbers, when you get to the large numbers, there's not enough space and it doesn't work anymore. So large numbers are weird cases" (Relaford-Doyle & Núñez, 2018, p. 248).

---

[76] The diagram comes from Relaford-Doyle and Núñez (2021, p. 6), reproduced with permission.

Relaford-Doyle and Núñez summarize:

> These responses all suggest that these participants believe that large num-
> bers may have qualitatively different properties than small numbers, such
> that rules that apply to small numbers may no longer work at larger magni-
> tudes. This is a reasonable conclusion to draw – in practice there are many
> differences between small and large numbers: small numbers . . . are encoun-
> tered more frequently, have simple numerical notation and lexical structure,
> and are easier to use in computations. However, this finding is surprising in
> that it is in opposition to the widely-held assumption in developmental psy-
> chology that 'mature' conceptualizations of natural number are consistent
> with the Dedekind-Peano axioms, in which the entire set of natural number
> is governed by the same logic. (Relaford-Doyle & Núñez, 2021, p. 14)

They conclude that "many undergraduates may possess non-normative concep-
tualizations of natural number" (Relaford-Doyle & Núñez, 2021, p. 18).

The subjects' remarks suggest that the "reasonable conclusion" they've
drawn is something like: the diagrammatic reasoning demonstrates the truth
of the target claim only for numbers to which it could be applied, numbers for
which there could be an array of dots, numbers up to which one could count –
what we might informally call "feasible" numbers. This idea generates a sorites
paradox – 1 is feasible, if n is feasible, so is $n + 1$, but 10^{70} is not – and nevertheless plays a leading role in Yessenin-Volpin's strict finitist program in the
foundations of mathematics (Yessenin-Volpin, 1970) and appears in computer
science as "feasible computation" (see, e.g., Dean, n.d.). These interconnections have been investigated philosophically by Dummett (1975) and more
recently and formally by Walter Dean (2018), but our concern here is with
the informal notion, the intuitive picture that appears to lie behind the reactions
of Relaford-Doyle and Núñez's subjects. Dean demonstrates the consistency
of this picture with a nonstandard model of arithmetic in which an "infinite
integer" plays the role of an unfeasible number. This isn't to say that these students – let's call them "feasibilists" – are referring to a non-standard model.
Theirs is an alternative intuitive picture on a psychological level analogous to
that of Parsons's Hilbertian notion,[77] not a model in the sense of model theory,
and that alternative intuition prompts them to disagree with those hewing to the
orthodox concept.

If these preliminary results are replicated and extended, one surprise would
be that the developmental story Relaford-Doyle and Núñez allude needs an
update: believing there's no largest number, appreciating the endlessness of

---

[77] Again, we're assuming that Parsons's Hilbertian intuitive picture is straightforwardly psychological, with no transcendental element. (Recall footnote 51.) That's why we take empirical
psychology to be relevant.

the sequence, 1, 2, 3, ..., isn't always enough to equip one with the notion of an orthodox omega sequence.[78,79] For Parsons's project, the surprise appears to be just what he feared: that our shared concept of natural number is not univocal; that it admits both feasibilist and more orthodox readings; that it doesn't include full mathematical induction in the usual sense. (The feasibilist apparently does think proof by induction works for the feasible portion of the number sequence.) Parsons's emphasis on the centrality of induction suggests that he might react by denying the feasibilist has a concept of natural number; he might restrict his circle of concept-sharing to those who've been trained on and internalized full mathematical induction (or perhaps come by it intuitively).[80]

This path seems uninviting. The subjects in these experiments are well-educated young people who operate successfully with numbers in their everyday and intellectual lives, so it doesn't seem plausible to claim that they lack the concept of natural number. Of course, Parsons is within his rights to limit the scope of his inquiry and to use the term "concept of natural number" as he chooses, but his Hilbertian intuitive picture is intended to answer to that concept, and the psychological description of the intuitive picture clearly bases it on our most fundamental thinking about numbers. The feasibilists among Relaford-Doyle and Núñez's subjects surely perceive figure/ground relations and temporal succession, surely experience space and time, so they must share the picture of the endless series of strings of strokes – $\|$, $\|\|$, $\|\|\|$, . . . – with their mathematical betters. Rather than painting the feasibilist as embracing an alternative to the Hilbertian picture, perhaps a better way to describe the situation is to say that we do all share that picture, but that the picture itself is vague in Parsons's sense, that it can be taken in (at least) two different ways, that it does, in a sense, "flicker in the distance." The threat of this kind of psychological

---

[78] The first author made something like this mistake, for example, in Maddy (2018, section 2), though she left open the possibility that our shared notion isn't fully determinate. Thanks to Jessica Gonzales, Christopher Mitsch, and Stella Moon (attendees at a seminar offered by Núñez at UCSD) for calling the work of Relaford-Doyle and Núñez to her attention.

[79] This would be particularly interesting developmentally, because it would locate a third and quite different linguistic, or perhaps better social, contribution to the mathematical conception of the natural numbers. In counting, the initially merely sing-song sequence of number words ends up providing a bridge between two primitive cognitive systems that we share with many other animals (one exact system for small numbers and one approximate system for larger numbers). After that, coming to realize there's no largest number depends on increasing dexterity with producing ever larger numerical expressions. This new and final third step would typically involve inculcation with mathematical induction.

[80] Relaford-Doyle and Núñez (2021, p. 1) begins with the observation that "Studies have repeatedly documented students' considerable difficulties in learning mathematical induction." Along the way, they note that even some students trained in mathematical induction understand it only at the "procedural" level – that is, as a sort of algebraic recipe – and not at the "conceptual" level that would allow them to recognize induction in the diagrammatic argument.

divergence isn't the sort of thing susceptible to the proving of theorems, about categoricity or anything else. But the empirical situation remains unsettled.

To sum up, if this general psychological question about our shared concept of number is what Parsons ultimately cares about, and if the experimental results hold, then his question – is it univocal? – would be answered in the negative. If the experimental results don't hold or if his interest is actually in the narrower question of the more learned concept of number, we're left with the mathematical question of how Kurt can define his isomorphism within the bounds of a first-order internal categoricity theorem – and the closest known mathematical results, Theorem 9 and Theorem 10, fall short of that goal. In the end, there seems room for doubt that our shared concept, Parsons's own Hilbertian intuition of the endless sequence of strokes, is as clear and determinate as we think it is. And if there is this room for doubt, formal categoricity theorems don't seem to be the kind of thing that might conceivably help. Given these open questions, both mathematical and philosophical, Parsons's appeal to categoricity arguments to establish "the uniqueness of the natural numbers" can't yet be judged a success.

6 Button and Walsh in "Categoricity" (2018)

6.1 What Do They Set Out to Accomplish?

As Kreisel points out (Section 4), anyone confident that the quantifiers of second-order logic are determinate should take the second-order version of Zermelo's categoricity theorem, Theorem 4, to show that CH has a determinate truth value – and, in fact, various observers make exactly this inference.[81] Tim Button and Sean Walsh in their 2018 book *Philosophy and Model Theory* (Button and Walsh, 2018) are not among them. Part B of that book, "Categoricity," includes an extended exploration of the possible bearing of categoricity on the status of CH, with analyses of both external and internal theorems. For most of the book, they adopt a philosophical perspective they call "modelism," but in Part B, they introduce an alternative, "internalism." Their official position is to endorse neither –

> We should emphasise right now . . . that we are not *advocating* internalism, any more than we were advocating modelism. Rather, we are presenting internalism in a speculative spirit. It is a fascinating position, worthy of attention, and we want to develop it as best we can. (Button & Walsh, 2018, p. 223)

---

[81] See, for example, Shapiro (2012, p. 105) and Hellman (1989, pp. 70–71).

– so our goal here is to examine their claims about what would follow if one were to adopt one perspective or the other.

Modelism, then, is a philosophical perspective on the nature of model theory, a branch of mathematics that takes place within set theory.[82] The modelist understands model theory as a piece of applied mathematics (cf. fluid dynamics) whose target phenomenon is the semantics of ordinary mathematical discourse (cf. the behavior of real world substances like water). More fully, model theory is to provide a workable account of the relations between the natural language of mathematics and a pre-theoretic metaphysics of structures that mathematics refers to (e.g., Shapiro, 2012) or concepts that mathematicians express (e.g., Hellman, 1989).[83] In this way, the natural language of actual mathematics is idealized to a formal language L and the structures mathematicians discuss to set-theoretic L-structures.[84] Faced with the modelist's appeal to Zermelo's result in its second-order form (Theorem 5), Button and Walsh reach the familiar conclusion:

> invoking [the second-order theorem] is simply *question-begging*, since the use of the full semantics simply *assumes* precisely what was at issue . . . in appealing to full second-order logic, the . . . modelist is simply out of the frying pan, and into another frying pan. (Button & Walsh, 2018, pp. 159–160)

---

[82] See, for example, Button and Walsh (2018, p. 145): "Model theory is officially implemented within set theory."

[83] See Button and Walsh (2018, sections 6.2 and 6.4, respectively). A remark on terminology: applied mathematicians often describe themselves as providing "models" for worldly phenomena, but it would obviously invite confusion to describe model theory as providing a model of the mathematical portion of natural language. We avoid this in the text with awkward circumlocutions like the one just employed – model theory provides a "workable account" – or it provides a "treatment" or some aspect of mathematical discourse is "idealized to" such and such. The reader is invited to interpret these passages as intending nothing other than "model" in sense of applied mathematics rather than that of model theory.

[84] Here, and in what follows, we elide the distinction between objects-modelism and concepts-modelism which Button and Walsh treat separately; reformulations of structure-talk into concept-talk should be relatively straightforward. Also, the modelism in question is "moderate," that is, one that "rejects all appeals to faculties of *mathematical intuition*, or anything similar" and appeals only to "human *faculties* . . . which could plausibly both have evolved within a species, and also could have developed within an individual creature as it grew from a fetus into an adult" (Button & Walsh, 2018, p. 42). Finally, these quotations all come in Button and Walsh's treatment of arithmetic rather than set theory, where the issue is the moderate modelist's appeal to the second-order version of Dedekind's categoricity theorem. When it comes to set theory, where appeal to the second-order version of Zermelo's theorem is what's at issue, they write that "we would re-run all the arguments [from the arithmetic context], occasionally replacing the phrase 'arithmetic' with 'set theory'. Flogging this dead horse would, though, be exhausting and unilluminating. So we shall pass over the corpse of moderate modelism without further ado" (Button & Walsh, 2018, pp. 181–182).

Internalism is then offered as an alternative perspective, from which internal categoricity theorems might gain better traction.

At the outset, all we're told about internalism is that it's a rejection of modelism and that it "relies heavily on deduction" (Button & Walsh, 2018, p. 223).[85] Later, the contrast between modelism and internalism is glossed in terms of their respective formalizations of a pre-theoretic claim like "there is a set-theoretic structure": the former offers "there is an X and a binary relation R on X such that $(X, R) \models \text{ZFC}^2$," while the latter formulates a second-order formula conjoining the axioms of ZFC^2 as direct claims about variables X and R and opts for the second-order statement $\exists X \exists R\, \text{ZFC}^2(X, R)$. If we imagine each of these as the antecedent of a categoricity theorem, this happily coincides with our characterization of the external/weakly internal distinction as a property of theorems in Section 2.3 – the former involves semantic notions and only mentions the axioms, while the latter involves no semantic notions and uses the axioms directly – so there's a tight connection between Button and Walsh's internalism and weakly internal categoricity theorems.

Beyond this, we're told that internalism is not if-thenism – because the antecedent is asserted unconditionally – not platonism – because no stand is taken on the nature of the pre-theoretic metaphysics of structures – and not logicism – because it has no epistemological ambitions.[86] And finally, "internalists need not fear the use of metalanguages . . . [they] only oppose *semantic* ascent" (Button & Walsh, 2018, p. 238) – so they're perfectly open to proof-theoretic metatheory. Still, for all this, internalism remains somewhat underspecified, a point to which we return in Section 6.3.

Given that Button and Walsh's project is exploratory, they can't be said to begin with a specific goal in mind, but they do end up with the conclusion that the mathematics they present . . .[87]

> . . . applies pressure to those who regard the continuum hypothesis as *indeterminate*. Indeed, it is not obvious how best to sustain that attitude (Button & Walsh, 2018, p. 255)

---

85 The deduction they have in mind is second order, what we've been writing as $\vdash_2$. Again (see footnote 84), the following attempt to characterize internalism is translated from the arithmetic context where it's explicit (Button & Walsh, 2018, chapter 10), to the set-theoretic context where it's presumably implicit (Button & Walsh, 2018, chapter 11).

86 See Button and Walsh (2018, pp. 236–237).

87 For the record, Button and Walsh have a second, "transcendental argument" for a limited conclusion that a leading argument for the indeterminateness of CH "walks a dangerously thin path between falsity and incoherence" (Button and Walsh, 2018, p. 256). Since this line of thought doesn't involve categoricity considerations, we leave it aside here.

This stops short of a straightforward affirmation that CH has a determinate truth value, despite leaning in that direction. We take this hedged conclusion as their goal, lay out the mathematics in Section 6.2, and evaluate its success in achieving that goal in Section 6.3.

6.2 What Do They Actually Do (or Can Be Done)?

We've seen that Button and Walsh take the semantic notions in Zermelo's Theorem 5 to render it ineffective in a defense of the determinateness of CH, so naturally what they now pursue is an internal categoricity theorem. We've also seen that their internalist is perfectly comfortable with syntactic second-order logic.[88] Here they obviously differ from Parsons, a difference rooted in their respective diagnoses of what goes wrong in an attempt to apply Zermelo's theorem to CH in this way: is the problem second-order logic itself or just the full semantics? We won't attempt to adjudicate this dispute, but the result is that Parsons sees internalness as an instrument for achieving a first-order result, while Button and Walsh see internalness as an end in itself. This is why Parsons needs a better version of Theorem 9 or Theorem 10, while Button and Walsh would be content with an internal theorem for ZF^2 that runs parallel to Theorem 8 for PA^2 – or rather, they want an internal theorem for ZF^2 running parallel to a version of Theorem 8 that's rephrased as a theorem of pure second-order logic.

At the risk of pedantry, let's make this explicit. First, suppose we've adapted the notational conventions laid out before Definition 3 for the case of PA^2 in the vocabulary $\{S, 0\}$ and new symbols $N_1, N_2, S_1, S_2, 0_1, 0_2$. Then, spelling out that definition, Theorem 8 becomes:

$$PA_1^{2(N_1)} \cup PA_2^{2(N_2)} \vdash_2 \exists F \, ISO(F, N_1, N_2). \tag{6.1}$$

As was noted in passing in Section 5.2, Definition 3 takes the form it does to allow for infinite theories, so the formulation for the current case can be simplified by exploiting the finiteness of PA^2. Let $\mathbf{PA}_1^{2(N_1)} = \bigwedge \{\phi^{(N_1)}(0_1, S_1): \phi(0, S) \in PA^2\} \cup \{N_1(0_1), \forall x(N_1(x) \rightarrow N_1(S_1(x)))\}$ and $\mathbf{PA}_2^{2(N_2)} = \bigwedge \{\phi^{(N_2)}(0_2, S_2): \phi(0, S) \in PA^2\} \cup \{N_2(0_2), \forall x(N_2(x) \rightarrow N_2(S_2(x)))\}$. Then (6.1) becomes:[89]

Theorem 11 (Theorem 8 restated, Internal categoricity for PA^2)

$$\vdash_2 \forall N_1, 0_1, S_1, N_2, 0_2, S_2((\mathbf{PA}_1^{2(N_1)} \wedge \mathbf{PA}_2^{2(N_2)}) \rightarrow \exists F \, ISO(F, N_1, N_2)).$$

---

[88] This is why they think Parsons should have settled for Theorem 6 (recall footnote 62).
[89] We treat the constant symbols $0, 0_1, 0_2$ as individual variables when they're quantified.

This is the arithmetic result that Button and Walsh hope to imitate for the case of set theory.[90]

Before leaving arithmetic, though, we should pause to ask precisely how Theorem 11 bears on the determinateness of arithmetic claims. From a modelist's perspective, a categoricity theorem in model theory has implications for the pre-theoretic realm of mathematical structures – namely, that the theory in question is satisfied by precisely one such structure[91] – and it follows that each of its claims has a determinate truth value.[92] But the internalist posits no such pre-theoretic metaphysics; the internal Theorem 11 involves no semantic notions. As Button and Walsh put it, "*no internal categoricity result can show that a theory pins down a unique $\mathcal{L}$-structure in the model-theorist's sense (even up-to-isomorphism)*" (Button & Walsh, 2018, p. 229, emphasis in the original). But an internal theorem can show what they call "intolerance."

To see how that goes, consider this immediate consequence of Theorem 11:

Corollary 2 *Suppose $\phi(0,S)$ is a second-order sentence in the vocabulary $\{0,S\}$. Then*

$$\vdash_2 \forall N_1, 0_1, S_1, N_2, 0_2, S_2((\mathbf{PA}_1^{2(N_1)} \wedge \mathbf{PA}_2^{2(N_2)}) \rightarrow$$
$$(\phi^{(N_1)}(0_1, S_1) \leftrightarrow \phi^{(N_2)}(0_2, S_2))).$$

Button and Walsh's "intolerance" follows:

Theorem 12 (Button & Walsh, 2018) ("Intolerance" of PA^2) *Suppose $\phi(0,S)$ is a second-order sentence in the vocabulary $\{0,S\}$. Then*

$$\vdash_2 \forall N, 0, S(\mathbf{PA}^{2(N)} \rightarrow \phi^{(N)}(0,S)) \vee \forall N, 0, S(\mathbf{PA}^{2(N)} \rightarrow \neg\phi^{(N)}(0,S))).$$

Proof: By Corollary 2,

$$\vdash_2 \forall N_1, 0_1, S_1, N_2, 0_2, S_2((\mathbf{PA}_1^{2(N_1)} \wedge \mathbf{PA}_2^{2(N_2)}) \rightarrow$$
$$(\phi^{(N_1)}(0_1, S_1) \vee \neg\phi^{(N_2)}(0_2, S_2))).$$

By rearranging quantifiers and connectives, we obtain

$$\vdash_2 \forall N_1 0_1 S_1(\mathbf{PA}_1^{2(N_1)} \rightarrow \phi^{(N_1)}(0_1, S_1)) \vee$$
$$\forall N_2 0_2 S_2(\mathbf{PA}_2^{2(N_2)} \rightarrow \neg\phi^{(N_2)}(0_2, S_2)))$$

from which the claim follows by change of bound variables.   □

---

[90] See Button and Walsh (2018, p. 228).

[91] If these pre-theoretic structures can be isomorphic without being identical, then: precisely one such structure up to isomorphism.

[92] On the assumption in the previous footnote: true in all such structures or false in all such structures – which is to say that each of its claims has a determinate truth value.

Another way to put this is:

Corollary 3 *If ϕ is a second-order sentence in the vocabulary $\{0, S\}$, then*

$$\mathbf{PA}_1^{2(N_1)} \cup \mathbf{PA}_2^{2(N_2)} \cup \{\phi^{(N_1)}(0_1, S_1), \neg\phi^{(N_2)}(0_2, S_2)\}$$

is deductively inconsistent.

Button and Walsh take this to place "pressure on the Algebraic Attitude toward arithmetic" (Button & Walsh, 2018, p. 236), that is, on the idea that arithmetic is not univocal.

This is the line of thought Button and Walsh want to see duplicated for the case of set theory. Categoricity will have to be replaced by quasi-categoricity – as in Theorem 5, the two models must be of the same height – but with that proviso, just such an internal theorem has been proved by the second author and Tong Wang (Väänänen & Wang, 2015). Begin with ZF^2 in the usual vocabulary $\{\in\}$.[93] Let E_1 and E_2 be binary relation symbols and X_1 and X_2 be unary relation symbols. If ϕ is a second-order sentence in the vocabulary $\{\in\}$, let $\phi(E_1)$ and $\phi(E_2)$ be translations of ϕ into the vocabularies $\{E_1\}$ and $\{E_2\}$, respectively, and let $\phi^{(X_1)}(E_1)$ and $\phi^{(X_2)}(E_2)$ be $\phi(E_1)$ and $\phi(E_2)$ be ϕ with its first- and second-order quantifiers relativized to X_1 and X_2, respectively. Once again exploiting finiteness, this time of ZF^2, let $\mathbf{ZF}^{2(X_1)}(E_1) = \bigwedge\{\phi^{(X_1)}(E_1): \phi(E_1) \in \mathrm{ZF}^2(E_1)\}$ and $\mathbf{ZF}^{2(X_2)}(E_2) = \bigwedge\{\phi^{(X_2)}(E_2): \phi(E_2) \in \mathrm{ZF}^2(E_2)\}$. Finally, let IA be the second-order sentence in the vocabulary $\{X_1, E_1, X_2, E_2\}$ which says – assuming the axioms of ZF^2 for (X_1, E_1) and (X_2, E_2) – that the classes of inaccessible cardinals in the sense of (X_1, E_1) and (X_2, E_2), respectively, are isomorphic, and let $\mathrm{ISO}((X_1, E_1), (X_2, E_2)))$ be the second-order sentence that says (X_1, E_1) and (X_2, E_2) are isomorphic. Then we have:

Theorem 13 (Väänänen & Wang, 2015)   (Internal quasi-categoricity of ZF^2)

$$\vdash_2 (\mathbf{ZF}^{2(X_1)}(E_1) \wedge \mathbf{ZF}^{2(X_2)}(E_2) \wedge IA) \rightarrow \mathrm{ISO}((X_1, E_1), (X_2, E_2)).$$

(Cf. Button & Walsh, 2018, p. 255.) As in the case of arithmetic (see Section 5.2), this implies Zermelo's categoricity theorem.

---

[93] Button and Walsh actually use Scott-Potter set theory, but this makes little difference for our purposes, so we stick with ZF^2 to maintain consistency. Urelements are similarly irrelevant, so for simplicity, we assume there are none.

The counterpart to Corollary 2 follows immediately:

Corollary 4   *Suppose ϕ is a second-order sentence in the vocabulary $\{\in\}$. Then*

$$\vdash_2 (\mathbf{ZF}^{2(X_1)}(E_1) \wedge \mathbf{ZF}^{2(X_2)}(E_2) \wedge IA) \to (\phi^{(X_1)}(E_1) \leftrightarrow \phi^{(X_2)}(E_2)).$$

The counterpart to arithmetic intolerance – the idea that every sentence is either true in all models or false in all models – requires fixing the number of inaccessibles, their order type. Any order type will do, so for the ultimate in simplicity, let IA_0 be the first-order sentence of set theory saying that there aren't any inaccessible cardinals, that every limit cardinal $> \omega$ is singular. Finally, let

$$\Gamma = \bigwedge(\mathrm{ZF}^2 \cup \{IA_0\}).$$

Then, if E is a new binary relation symbol and X a new unary relation symbol, we have

Theorem 14 (Button & Walsh, 2018)   ("Intolerance" of ZF^2) *Suppose ϕ is a second-order sentence in the vocabulary $\{\in\}$. Then*

$$\vdash_2 \forall X, E(\Gamma^{(X)}(E) \to \phi^{(X)}(E)) \vee \forall X, E(\Gamma^{(X)}(E) \to \neg\phi^{(X)}(E)).$$

Proof: By Corollary 4,

$$\vdash_2 \forall X_1, E_1, X_2, E_2((\Gamma^{(X_1)}(E_1) \wedge \Gamma^{(X_2)}(E_2)) \to (\phi^{(X_1)}(E_1) \vee \neg\phi^{(X_2)}(E_2))).$$

By rearranging quantifiers and connectives, we obtain

$$\vdash_2 \forall X_1, E_1(\Gamma^{(X_1)}(E_1) \to \phi^{(X_1)}(E_1)) \vee \forall X_2, E_2(\Gamma^{(X_2)}(E_2) \to \neg\phi^{(X_2)}(E_2))),$$

from which the claim follows by change of bound variables.   □ Once again, "intolerance" can be rephrased:

Corollary 5   *If ϕ is a second-order sentence in vocabulary $\{\in\}$, then the theory*

$$\{\Gamma^{(X_1)}(E_1), \Gamma^{(X_2)}(E_2), \phi^{(X_1)}(E_1), \neg\phi^{(X_2)}(E_2)\}$$

is deductively inconsistent.

From this, Button and Walsh draw the expected conclusion:

> The present observation applies ... pressure to those who regard the continuum hypothesis as *indeterminate*. Indeed, it is not obvious how best to sustain that attitude, in the face of this deductive inconsistency. (Button & Walsh, 2018, p. 255)

We examine this claim in Section 6.3.

Theorem 13 is both weakly internal and pure; of the desiderata present in Parsons's discussion, it fails only to be first-order. Of course, this doesn't trouble Button and Walsh, but it's still worth observing that internal categoricity and its consequences can be carried over to first-order ZF. The source of categoricity is actually more transparent in the first-order than in the second-order context because blanket appeal to the second-order comprehension axiom is replaced by explicit, targeted features of the first-order separation and replacement schemas.

To see this, begin with first-order ZF in the vocabulary $\{\in\}$ and use the notation ZF(E) for the result of replacing $\in$ with a binary relation symbol E. Now suppose that E_1 and E_2 are new binary relation symbols, X_1 and X_2 are new unary relation symbols, and π is a new unary function symbol. If $\phi(E)$ is a sentence in the vocabulary $\{E\}$, let $\phi^{(X)}(E)$ be $\phi(E)$ with the first-order quantifiers relativized to X. Now let $\mathrm{ZF}^{(X_1)}(E_1)$ consist of all $\phi^{(X_1)}(E_1)$, where $\phi \in \mathrm{ZF}$, allowing in the separation and replacement schemas formulas from the vocabulary $\{X_1, E_1, X_2, E_2, \pi, \in\}$ with unrestricted (i.e., not relativized to X_1) quantifiers – and similarly $\mathrm{ZF}^{(X_2)}(E_2)$. Let IO_π be a first-order sentence of the vocabulary $\{X_1, E_1, X_2, E_2, \pi, \in\}$ saying – assuming the axioms ZF for (X_1, E_1) and (X_2, E_2) – that π is an isomorphism between the ordinals of (X_1, E_1) and the ordinals of (X_2, E_2). Finally, given a formula $\phi(x, y)$, let $\mathrm{ISO}_\phi((X_1, E_1), (X_2, E_2))$ be a first-order sentence that says – again assuming the axioms ZF for (X_1, E_1) and (X_2, E_2) – that $\phi(x, y)$ defines an isomorphism between (X_1, E_2) and (X_2, E_2), extending π. Then

Theorem 15 (Internal quasi-categoricity of ZF) *There is a first-order formula* $\phi = \phi(x, y)$ *of set theory such that*

$$\mathrm{ZF} \cup \mathrm{ZF}^{(X_1)}(E_1) \cup \mathrm{ZF}^{(X_2)}(E_2) \cup \{\mathrm{IO}_\pi\} \vdash \mathrm{ISO}_\phi((X_1, E_1), (X_2, E_2)).$$

The proof is as in Väänänen (2019).[94] Here the axioms for (X_1, E_1) and (X_2, E_2) are shifted to the left side of the turnstile because they are infinite in number, but this is trivial. Theorem 15 also has an extra ZF on the left side, like the extra PA in Theorem 9, but this is less troublesome here, where we aren't worried about Kurt's epistemic limitations. More to the current point, what fundamentally differentiates Theorem 15 from the second-order Theorem 13 is, as advertized, the mechanism by which the crucial links between the (X_1, E_1) and (X_2, E_2) are forged: in the first-order theorem, the key is allowing the vocabulary of one into

---

[94] Martin (2018) can be read as giving an informal proof of something like this theorem. A claim resembling Theorem 16 is formulated (without proof) in the appendix to McGee (1997).

the axiom schemas of the other; in the second-order theorem, these specifics
are masked in the undifferentiated Comprehension Axioms.

As with arithmetic, the ZF on the left side can be eliminated if we assume
that the domains of the two versions of ZF are the same and comprehensive.
An extra assumption like IO_π is now unnecessary, but ISO_ϕ needs modifica-
tion: given a formula $\phi(x,y)$, let AUT_ϕ be the first-order sentence which says
that $\phi(x,y)$ defines an automorphism between the binary predicates E_1 and E_2,
again assuming the axioms ZF for E_1 and E_2. Let $ZF(E, E')$ be ZF with E as the
membership relation, but with separation and replacement schemas allowing
formulas from the vocabulary $\{E, E'\}$. Then

Theorem 16 (Väänänen, 2019)   *There is a first-order formula $\phi = \phi(x,y)$ of
set theory such that*

$$ZF(E_1, E_2) \cup ZF(E_2, E_1) \vdash AUT_\phi(E_1, E_2).$$

Here we have our counterpart to Theorem 10.

As in the aftermath of Theorem 13, there's this immediate consequence:

Corollary 6   *If ψ is a first-order sentence in the vocabulary $\{\in\}$, then*

$$ZF(E_1, E_2) \cup ZF(E_2, E_1) \vdash \psi(E_1) \leftrightarrow \psi(E_2).$$

And a new version of Button and Walsh's intolerance then follows. Let
$ZF_n(E, E')$ be the conjunction of the first n axioms of $ZF(E, E')$ under some
natural enumeration. Then

Theorem 17 (Button & Walsh, 2018)   *("Intolerance" of ZF) There is a natural number n such that if ψ is a first-order sentence in the vocabulary $\{\in\}$,
then*

$$\vdash (ZF_n(E_1, E_2) \rightarrow \psi(E_1)) \vee (ZF_n(E_2, E_1) \rightarrow \neg\psi(E_2)).$$

Proof: By Theorem 15 there is an n such that

$$ZF_n(E_1, E_2) \cup ZF_n(E_2, E_1) \vdash AUT_\phi(E_1, E_2).$$

Relying on $AUT_\phi(E_1, E_2)$, induction on ψ shows that

$$\vdash (ZF_n(E_1, E_2) \wedge ZF_n(E_2, E_1)) \rightarrow (\psi(E_1) \leftrightarrow \psi(E_2)).$$

It follows by propositional logic that

$$\vdash (ZF_n(E_1, E_2) \rightarrow \psi(E_1)) \vee (ZF_n(E_2, E_1) \rightarrow \neg\psi(E_2)). \qquad \square$$

And finally,

Corollary 7 *If ψ is a first-order sentence of the vocabulary $\{\in\}$, then the theory*

$$\{ZF(E_1, E_2), ZF(E_2, E_1), \psi(E_1), \neg\psi(E_2)\} \tag{6.2}$$

is deductively inconsistent.

6.3 Do They (or Can They) Accomplish What They Set Out to Do?

To recap, Button and Walsh have argued that semantic second-order logic can't underpin a persuasive defense of the determinateness of CH, so the question is whether the syntactic second-order logic of the internal categoricity theorems of Section 6.2 can do better. They note that "no internal categoricity result can show that a theory pins down a unique L-structure in the model-theorist's sense (even up-to-isomorphism)" (Button & Walsh, 2018, p. 229), and for that reason, these results provide no direct comfort to the modelist. Still, they argue, taking the internalist's perspective, Theorems 13 and 14 and their corollaries make concern over the determinateness of CH difficult to sustain.[95] Here it's worth noting that Theorem 14 only says that a certain disjunction is provable in syntactic second-order logic, which of course doesn't mean that either disjunct need be provable. From this theorem, the internalist can infer that any model of the second-order axioms must satisfy the disjunction. Continuing the internalist's line of thought, this can only mean that any Henkin model satisfies it – which obviously leaves open the possibility that some such models satisfy one and some the other disjunct. This would certainly appear sufficient to sustain reasonable concern about the determinateness of CH. (We suggest below that this isn't the true source of internalistic worries about CH.)

In any case, Button and Walsh's actual discussion takes a different approach to their goal, attempting not to establish the determinateness of CH but to defuse the inclination to think otherwise:

> It is doubtful that we can understand the claim that there are multiple 'equally preferable' models, some of which satisfy the continuum hypothesis and others which do not, and hence the supposed *motivation* for thinking that the continuum hypothesis is indeterminate. (Button & Walsh, 2018, p. 256)

---

[95] Recall the quotation from Button and Walsh (2018, p. 255), displayed at the end of Section 6.1.

What they have in mind here is a concern about CH arising from the fact that ZF^2 admits non-isomorphic Henkin models, and they claim that this argument has been undercut.[96] Of course, this is a modelist motivation: the model-theoretic fact of non-isomorphic models is taken to reflect the existence of non-isomorphic pre-theoretic metaphysical structures. But a modelist case for the determinateness of CH has already been rejected, and this argument from non-isomorphic models to metaphysical structures is not one any self-respecting internalist would make. If an internalist were concerned about the status of CH, it would be for other reasons, perhaps reasons not assuaged by categoricity, intolerance, or deductive inconsistency.

This points to a more fundamental problem: Button and Walsh haven't given internalism a fair hearing, or so we claim. If modelism is an understanding of model theory as an applied mathematical treatment of the semantics of ordinary mathematical discourse, then internalism should be an understanding of proof theory as an applied mathematical treatment of the proving activity of mathematicians – perhaps a better counterpart to the term "modelism" would be "proofism."[97] These two represent the poles of "mathematics as descriptive activity" vs. "mathematics as proving activity," depending on which is taken as fundamental. The modelist will regard proving activity as instrumentally important, as epistemology, a way of gaining insight into the pre-theoretic structures. The proofist will regard ordinary mathematical language as meaningful, but Austin and Wittgenstein have taught us that a discourse can be meaningful without being referential. The proofist's practice is purely syntactic in the sense that it involved no appeal to a subject matter (and in particular, no appeal to the modelist's structures).[98]

---

[96] See Button and Walsh (2018, pp. 255–256). It seems this undercutting is largely based on the "transcendental" considerations of their chapter 9, rather than Intolerance and Deductive Inconsistency. (Recall footnote 87.)

[97] This parallel has its limits, two of which we note for the record, one here and another in footnote 98. First is the observation that the applied math story is more plausible in the case of proof theory than of model theory. A modelist, noting that first-order PA has non-standard models, draws as an immediate consequence that the pre-theoretic metaphysics includes corresponding non-standard structures, but applied mathematics doesn't work that way: the continuity of an ideal fluid is known not to carry over to actual water; applied mathematicians take great care to determine which aspects of their treatments correspond to the worldly situation and which don't, to determine which idealizations are safe in which contexts. Likewise for the proofist: the existence of a proof-theoretic "proof" isn't taken as conclusive evidence of the possibility, let alone the actuality, of a real world proof. This suggests that proof theory is answerable to a worldly phenomenon capable of pushing back, while model theory is not.

[98] The second limitation of the parallel between the modelist and the proofist concerns their views of proof theory and model theory, respectively. Both regard proof theory as an applied mathematical account of real world proving activity. Where they differ is on model theory, which the modelist also sees as an applied mathematical account, this time of the semantics of real world mathematical discourse. The proofist doesn't think real world mathematical discourse

Much could be said about this proofism,[99] but for our purposes, the central point is that "does CH have a determinate truth value?" is an essentially semantic question, not the sort of thing the proofist would (or could) ask. If we fully commit to the proofist perspective, the salient question about CH isn't whether it has a determinate truth value – the modelist's truth and existence simply aren't part of this discourse. The question that arises for the proofist is whether the set-theoretic community will ever hit upon an axiom (or other unforseen type of development) with sufficient mathematical advantages to merit adoption – and which implies CH or implies ¬CH. (The worry that this may never happen would be the source of a proofist's concern about the status of CH.) Perhaps not coincidentally, this is what many set theorists who engage with foundations are actively trying to do, whatever their metaphysical or semantics beliefs might be. The ultimate fate of this endeavor remains uncertain, but one point is clear: internal categoricity theorems provide no assurance of success.

We conclude that Button and Walsh have not succeeded in establishing that internalist (proofist) concerns over the status of CH are "difficult to sustain."

7 Conclusion

We've now surveyed five different attempts to put categoricity results to philosophical use. The efforts of Dedekind, Zermelo, and Kreisel we take to have been successful; those of Parsons and Button-Walsh less so. Can any general moral be drawn from these observations? Is there a distinguishing feature that accounts for the disparity between the first group and the second?

One obvious difference is that Parsons and Button-Walsh focus on internal theorems and carefully police the background theory in which they're

---

has a semantics in the modelist's sense – it's not referential, it isn't out to describe or discover truths about some robust subject matter. It's simply a practice of devising and deploying mathematically rich concepts and theories, some in reaction to (presumably) shared intuitive pictures, some for purely mathematical ends, some for the purposes of natural science. Likely due to the structure of human cognition (see, e.g., Maddy, 2018), these concepts and theories are expressed in terms of things with properties, things in relations, and the like. Model theory takes place within this practice, within the imagined ontology of the practice, as an account of the relations between a formalized version of ordinary language of the discourse and the things the theory itself has imagined. So a formal language, L, corresponds to ordinary mathematical discourse, just as the modelist has it, but the corresponding L-structure, made of elements of the imagined ontology, corresponds to nothing real. This ploy has foundational uses – in independence proofs, for just one example – and its own particular interest as a branch of mathematics in its own right.

[99] Some of it is said in footnotes 97 and 98. For the record, proofism isn't a brand of intuitionism: the human activity being modeled is the ordinary practice of classical mathematics (where, e.g., excluded middle and non-constructive proofs are freely allowed), and the proof theory serving as a model is ordinary classical proof theory. Interested readers are referred to the "Enhanced If-thenism" of Maddy (2022) or the "Arealism" of Maddy (2011).

proved, for the sake of a kind of purity: first-order PA (Parsons) or syntactic second-order logic (Button-Walsh). These features or their absence simply aren't salient for the earlier authors, so it's worth asking what explains their centrality for Parsons and Button-Walsh. The answer seems to lie in the fact that their respective goals are qualitatively different from those of their predecessors. Parsons is out to show the determinateness of our concept of natural number, the uniqueness of the structure it purportedly describes (up to isomorphism). Button and Walsh hope to establish that it's at least extremely difficult to maintain that CH lacks a determinate truth value. Both these projects concern an ambient pre-theoretic metaphysics that stands in relation to ordinary mathematical discourse (referred to, expressed by). In contrast, the efforts of Dedekind, Zermelo, and Kreisel are closely tied to mathematical ambitions: Dedekind demonstrates that the concept of natural number can be characterized without appeal to spatio-temporal intuition; Zermelo shows how the set-theoretic axioms, especially Foundation, generate a streamlined and fruitful characterization of the universe of sets; Kreisel points out that the newly established independence of CH is of a new variety, qualitatively different from that of previous examples like large cardinal axioms. These are all significant philosophical advances, but none concern the semantics of ordinary mathematical discourse or its purported, pre-theoretic subject matter.

One last question: if these new pure internal categoricity theorems don't establish what recent writers had hoped, are they without foundational significance? Perhaps unsurprisingly, we think the first-order theorems do make an important philosophical point: an outcome that was thought to require second-order resources – namely, categoricity theorems – can actually be achieved by suitable first-order means. What seems to be crucial is a link between the languages of the two relevant models – whether hidden in the second-order comprehension axioms of Theorems 11 and 13 or explicit in the assumptions of Theorems 9 and 15. This is a useful discovery, which supports our general moral: a bit of mathematics that fails at one task might succeed (and even be aimed) at another.

References

Barwise, K. J. (1972). The Hanf number of second order logic. *Journal of Symbolic Logic, 37*, 588–594. https://doi.org/10.2307/2272748.

Benacerraf, P., & Putnam, H. (Eds. 1983). *Philosophy of Mathematics: Selected readings* (2nd ed.). Cambridge University Press, Cambridge.

Bernays, P. (1935). On platonism in mathematics, (Translated from the French by C. Parsons, Benacerraf and Putnam (1983), pp. 258–271)

Boolos, G. (1971). The iterative conception of set. Reprinted in Benacerraf and Putnam (1983), pp. 496–502. https://doi.org/10.2307/2025204.

Bowler, N. (2019). Foundations for the working mathematician, and for their computer. In S. Centrone, D. Kant, and D. Sarikaya (Eds.), *Reflections on the Foundations of Mathematics: Univalent Foundations, Set Theory and General Thoughts* (pp. 399–416). Springer, Cham. https://doi.org/10.1007/978-3-030-15655-8_18.

Button, T., & Walsh, S. (2018). *Philosophy and Model Theory*. Oxford University Press, Oxford. https://doi.org/10.1093/oso/9780198790396.001.0001 (With a historical appendix by Wilfrid Hodges).

Chu, J., Cheung, P., Schneider, R., Sullivan, J., & Barner, D. (2020). Counting to infinity: Does learning the syntax of the count list predict knowledge that numbers are infinite? *Cognitive Science*, 44, 1–30.

Corcoran, J. (1980). Categoricity. *History and Philosophy of Logic, 1*, 187–207. https://doi.org/10.1080/01445348008837010.

Dean, W. (2021). Computational complexity theory. In E. N. Zalta (Ed.), *The Stanford Encyclopedia of Philosophy* (Fall 2021 ed.). https://plato.stanford.edu/archives/fall2021/entries/computationalcomplexity.

Dean, W. (2018). Strict finitism, feasibility, and the sorites. *Review of Symbolic Logic, 11*(2), 295–346. https://doi.org/10.1017/S1755020318000163.

Dedekind, R. (1890). Letter to Keferstein. (Translated from German by H. Wang and S. Bauer-Mengelberg. van Heijenoort, 1967, pp. 99–103)

Dedekind, R. (1872). *Continuity and irrational Numbers. (Translated from German by W. Beeman and W. Ewald. Ewald (2005), pp. 766–779.)*

Dedekind, R. (1888). Was sind und was sollen die zahlen?. (Translated from German by W. Beeman and W. Ewald. Ewald (2005), pp. 790–833.)

Detlefsen, M., & Arana, A. (2011). Purity of methods. *Philosophers' Imprint, 11.*

Dummett, M. (1963). The philosophical significance of Gödel's theorem *Ratio, 5, 140–155.* Reprinted in Dummett (1978), pp.186–201.

Dummett, M. (1967). Platonism. In Dummett (1978), pp. 202–214.

Dummett, M. (1975). Wang's paradox. *Synthese, 30*(3–4), 201–32. Reprinted in Dummett (1978), pp. 248–268. https://doi.org/10.1007/BF00485048.

Dummett, M. (1978), *Truth and Other Enigmas.* Harvard University Press, Cambridge, MA.

Ebbinghaus, H.- D. (2007). *Ernst Zermelo: An Approach to his Life and Work.* (In cooperation with V. Peckhaus) Springer, Berlin.

Enderton, H. (1977). *Elements of Set Theory.* Academic Press, Amsterdam.

Ewald, W. B. (Ed. 2005). *From Kant to Hilbert: A Source Book in the Foundations of Mathematics*, volume 2. Oxford University Press, Oxford.

Feferman, S. (1972). Infinitary properties, local functors, and systems of ordinal functions. In W. Hodges (Ed.) *Conference in Mathematical Logic: London '70.* Lecture notes in mathematics (Vol. 255, pp. 63–97).

Field, H. (2001). Postscript to "Which undecidable mathematical sentences have determinate truth values?." In H. Field, *Truth and the Absence of Fact* (pp. 351–360). Oxford University Press, Oxford.

Hellman, G. (1989). *Mathematics without Numbers: Towards a Modal-structural Interpretation.* Oxford University Press, Oxford.

Hilbert, D. (1926). On the infinite. In J. van Heijenoort (1967) (pp. 369–392).

Kanamori, A. (2010a). Introduction to Zermelo (1930a). In Zermelo (2010), pp. 432–433.

Kanamori, A. (2010b). Introduction to Zermelo (1930c). In Zermelo (2010), pp. 390–399.

Kreisel, G. (1967). Informal rigour and completeness proofs. In I. Lakatos (Ed.), *Problems in the Philosophy of Mathematics* (pp. 138–157). North-Holland, Amsterdam.

Kreisel, G. (1969). Two notes on the foundations of set-theory. *Dialectica, 23*(2), 93–114. https://doi.org/10.1111/j.1746-8361.1969.tb01184.x.

Lavine, S. (1994). *Understanding the Infinite.* Harvard University Press, Cambridge, MA.

Lavine, S. (1999). Skolem was wrong. Unpublished.

Maddy, P. (2011). *Defending the Axioms: On the Philosophical Foundations of Set Theory,* Oxford University Press, Oxford. https://doi.org/10.1093/acprof:oso/9780199596188.001.0001.

Maddy, P. (2018). Psychology and the a priori sciences. In S. Bangu (Ed.), *Naturalizing Mathematical Knowledge: Approaches From Philosophy, Psychology and Cognitive Science*, pp. 15–29, Routledge, New York. Reprinted in P. Maddy, *A Plea for Natural Philosophy and Other Essays* (pp. 262–293). Oxford University Press, New York.

Maddy, P. (2022). Enhanced if-thenism. In P. Maddy, *A Plea for Natural Philosophy and Other Essays* (pp. 262–293). Oxford University Press, New York.

Martin, D. (2018). *Completeness or incompleteness of basic mathematical concepts* (draft). www.math.ucla.edu/dam/booketc/efi.pdf

McGee, V. (1997). How we learn mathematical language. *Philosophical Review*, *106*(1), 35–68. https://doi.org/10.2307/2998341.

Moore, G. H. (1982). *Zermelo's Axiom of Choice: Its Origins, Development, and Influence.* Springer, New York. https://doi.org/10.1007/978-1-4613-9478-5.

Parsons, C. (1990). The uniqueness of the natural numbers. *Iyyun: The Jerusalem Philosophical Quarterly*, *39*, 13–44. http://www.jstor.org/stable/23350653.

Parsons, C. (2008). *Mathematical Thought and its Objects.* Cambridge University Press, Cambridge.

Quine, W. V. (1970). *Philosophy of Logic.* (Sixth printing) Prentice-Hall, Englewood Cliffs, NJ.

Reck, E. (2003). Dedekind's structuralism: An interpretation and partial defense. *Synthese*, *137*, 369–419.

Relaford-Doyle, J., & Núñez, R. (2017). When does a "visual proof by induction" serve a proof-like function in mathematics. In A. Howes and T. Tenbrink (Eds.), *Proceedings of the 39th Annual Meeting of the Cognitive Science Society* (pp. 1004–1009). Cognitive Science Society, London.

Relaford-Doyle, J., & Núñez, R. (2018). Beyond Peano: Looking into the unnaturalness of natural numbers. In S. Bangu (Ed.), *Naturalizing Logicomathematical Knowledge* (pp. 234–251). Routledge, New York.

Relaford-Doyle, J., & Núñez, R. (2021). Characterizing students' conceptual difficulties with mathematical induction using visual proofs. *International Journal of Research in Undergraduate Mathematics Education*, *7*, 1–20.

Shapiro, S. (1991). *Foundations without Foundationalism: a Case for Second-order Logic.* Oxford University Press, New York.

Shapiro, S. (2012). Higher-order logic or set theory: A false dilemma. *Philosophia Mathematica*, *20*(3), 305–323. https://doi.org/10.1093/philmat/nks002.

Sieg, W., & Morris, R. (2018). Dedekind's structuralism: Creating concepts and deriving theorems. In E. Reck (Ed.) *Logic, Philosophy of Mathematics and their History* (pp. 251–301). College, London.

Simpson, S. G., & Yokoyama, K. (2013). Reverse mathematics and Peano categoricity. *Annals of Pure and Applied Logic*, *164*(3), 284–293. https://doi.org/10.1016/j.apal.2012.10.014.

Spelke, E. (2000). Core knowledge. *American Psychologist*, *55*, 1233–1243.

Väänänen, J. (2019). An extension of a theorem of Zermelo. *Bulletin of Symbolic Logic*, *25*(2), 208–212. https://doi.org/10.1017/bsl.2019.15.

Väänänen, J. (2021). Tracing internal categoricity. *Theoria*, *87*, 986–1000.

Väänänen, J., & Wang, T. (2015). Internal categoricity in arithmetic and set theory. *Notre Dame Journal Formal Logic*, *56*(1), 121–134. http://dx.doi.org/10.1215/00294527-2835038.

van Heijenoort, J. (Ed. 1967). *From Frege to Gödel: A Source Book in Mathematical Logic, 1879–1931*. Harvard University Press, Cambridge, MA.

Walmsley, J. (2002). Categoricity and indefinite extensibility. *Proceedings of the Aristotelian Society*, *102*(3), 217–235.

Wang, H. (1974). *The concept of set*. Reprinted in (Benacerraf & Putnam, 1983, pp. 530–570).

Weston, T. (1976). Kreisel, the continuum hypothesis and second order set theory. *Journal of Philosophical Logic*, *5*(2), 281–298. https://doi.org/10.1007/BF00248732.

Wittgenstein, L. (1978). *Remarks on the Foundations of Mathematics* (Revised ed.) (Edited by G. H. vonWright, R. Rhees and G. E. M. Anscombe, Translated from the German by G. E. M. Anscombe). MIT Press, Cambridge, MA.

Yessenin-Volpin, A. S. (1970). The ultra-intuitionistic criticism and the antitraditional program for foundations of mathematics. In R. E. Vesley, A. Kino, and J. Myhill (Eds.) *Intuitionism and Proof Theory (Proceedings of the Summer Conference at Buffalo, NY., 1968)*. North Holland, Amsterdam (pp. 3–45).

Zermelo, E. (1908a). A new proof of the possibility of a well-ordering. (Translated from German by S. Bauer-Mengelberg. Reprinted in van Heijenoort (1967), pp. 183–198, and in Zermelo (2010), pp. 120–159). https://doi.org/10.1007/BF01450054.

Zermelo, E. (1908b). Investigations in the foundations of set theory I. (Translated from German by S. Bauer-Mengelberg. Reprinted in van Heijenoort (1967), pp. 200–215, and in Zermelo (2010), pp. 188–229). https://doi.org/10.1007/BF01449999.

Zermelo, E. (1930a). Report to the emergency association of German science. (Translated from German by E. de Pellegrin. In Zermelo (2010), pp. 434–443).

Zermelo, E. (1930b). On the set-theoretic model. (Translated from German by E. de Pellegrin. In Zermelo (2010), pp. 446–453).

Zermelo, E. (1930c). On boundary numbers and domains of sets. (Translated from German by E. de Pellegrin. Reprinted in Zermelo (2010), pp. 400–430).

Zermelo, E. (2010). *Collected Works*, volume I. (H.-D Ebbinghaus and A. Kanamori, Eds. Springer, Berlin). https://doi.org/10.1007/978-3-540-79384-7.

Acknowledgments

The first author would like to thank Charles Leitz, Chris Mitsch, Stella Moon, Jeffrey Schatz, and Evan Sommers for helpful comments on an earlier draft. The second author would like to thank the Academy of Finland (grant number 322795). This project has received funding from the European Research Council (ERC) under the European Union's Horizon 2020 research and innovation programme (grant agreement number 101020762). Thanks also to the anonymous referees for their helpful reports.

Cambridge Elements $\equiv$

The Philosophy of Mathematics

Penelope Rush

University of Tasmania

From the time Penny Rush completed her thesis in the philosophy of mathematics (2005), she has worked continuously on themes around the realism/anti-realism divide and the nature of mathematics. Her edited collection *The Metaphysics of Logic* (Cambridge University Press, 2014), and forthcoming essay 'Metaphysical Optimism' (*Philosophy Supplement*), highlight a particular interest in the idea of reality itself and curiosity and respect as important philosophical methodologies.

Stewart Shapiro

The Ohio State University

Stewart Shapiro is the O'Donnell Professor of Philosophy at The Ohio State University, a Distinguished Visiting Professor at the University of Connecticut, and a Professorial Fellow at the University of Oslo. His major works include *Foundations without Foundationalism* (1991), *Philosophy of Mathematics: Structure and Ontology* (1997), *Vagueness in Context* (2006), and *Varieties of Logic* (2014). He has taught courses in logic, philosophy of mathematics, metaphysics, epistemology, philosophy of religion, Jewish philosophy, social and political philosophy, and medical ethics.

About the Series

This Cambridge Elements series provides an extensive overview of the philosophy of mathematics in its many and varied forms. Distinguished authors will provide an up-to-date summary of the results of current research in their fields and give their own take on what they believe are the most significant debates influencing research, drawing original conclusions.

Cambridge Elements ⁼

The Philosophy of Mathematics

Printed in the United States
by Baker & Taylor Publisher Services